THE AUTHOR'S GUIDE TO MARKETING BOOKS ON AMAZON

ROB EAGAR

The Author's Guide to
Marketing Books on Amazon

Published by Wildfire Marketing
www.StartaWildfire.com

Requests to publish work from this book should be sent to:
Rob@StartaWildfire.com

Cover design by Ron Dylnicki

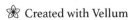 Created with Vellum

CONTENTS

Endorsements   v
My Free Gift for You   vii
Preface   ix
Introduction   xv

1. Master Your Amazon Book Detail Page   1
2. Four Ways to Get Customer Reviews for Free   43
3. Maximize Your Author Central Account   57
4. Amazon's Secret Marketing Back Door   75
5. Understanding the Amazon Best Sellers Rank   87
6. Use Amazon Ads to Your Advantage   103
7. How to Build Your Email List Using Amazon   127

Conclusion   149
My Free Gift for You   153
About Rob Eagar   155
Get Expert Help for Your Books   159
Other Books by Rob Eagar   161

ENDORSEMENTS

"I recommend Rob Eagar to any author looking to take their book campaign to a higher level."

Dr. Gary Chapman - #1 *New York Times* bestselling author of *The Five Love Languages*

"I give Rob Eagar my highest recommendation. If you want to increase book sales, make him the first person you hire."

Lysa TerKeurst - 5-time *New York Times* bestselling author

"Rob Eagar gets great results and strategically places authors in the right spaces. I'm happy with what Rob did for me, and I highly recommend him."

Dr. John Townsend - *New York Times* bestselling author of *Boundaries*

"Rob Eagar provided effective marketing strategy and worked closely with my team to execute new promotional ideas. I highly recommend Rob."

DeVon Franklin - CEO of Franklin Entertainment and *New York Times* bestselling author

"Rob Eagar knows how to use words and has fine penmanship. You should really listen to him."

His Mother - English major who taught Rob to speak clearly

"Rob revolutionized how I market my novels and connect with readers. His Book Marketing Master Class gave me more fantastic ideas than I knew what to do with."

Dani Pettrey - Bestselling novelist with over 300,000 copies sold

"Rob Eagar's expertise helped me develop a new brand and create an exciting new website. It was beyond my expectations and included everything I asked for and more."

Wanda Brunstetter - 6-time *New York Times* bestselling novelist with over 10 million copies sold

MY FREE GIFT FOR YOU

Get 3 e-books to help jumpstart your book sales for FREE:

Find Readers and Sell Books on a Shoestring Budget

Mastering Book Hooks for Authors

The Ultimate Book Marketing Plan Template for Authors

Join my email newsletter and get these 3 e-books. Each resource can be downloaded as a file to your computer or added to any e-reader device. You will also receive my weekly e-newsletter packed with expert marketing advice for authors.

Download these 3 e-books for free today at:

https://www.startawildfire.com/free-ebooks-ag

PREFACE

If you've written a book, then by definition you are considered an "author." Do you know what that title really means? Today, the word "author" means you are one of the bravest souls on the planet or one of the most unrealistic dreamers in our society. Why? Consider the incredible challenge that every modern author must face:

- Over 1,000,000 new books are published every year
- A book has less than a 1% change of getting stocked on a bookstore shelf
- The average U.S. nonfiction book sells less than 250 copies per year

Source: *https://www.bkconnection.com/the-10-awful-truths-about-book-publishing*

With statistics like these, it's a wonder anyone decides to write a book. Yet, here you are. You're reading this guide because you're a writer seeking to beat the odds. You believe in yourself even though the numbers say success is nearly impossible. Or, you're just plain crazy, but crazy enough to follow your dreams.

I'm an author, too. Just like you, I chose to make a career out of writing books, even when my friends and family thought I had lost my mind. I entered the publishing world in 2002, before the luxury of fancy technology, such as social media, blogging, or live webcasts. Amazon was still a tiny company that no one thought would survive.

I am also a maverick. I decided to self-publish my first book before it was cool to be an "indie" author. You could call me one of the original self-publishing success stories. I was just a normal guy who had never written a book, had no fan base, and had no idea what an "author platform" meant. However, I did possess a business education, 10 years of experience working in the corporate world, and a burning desire to share a message that I knew could help people.

Armed with a headstrong determination in the face of my doubters, I tried every possible tactic available to sell my books. I started small, but my persistence and hunger for marketing knowledge paid off. Within a few years, I sold over 13,000 copies on my own, built a nationwide following, and created an email list with over 8,000 subscribers. Public speaking was widely available at the time, and I spoke at over 170 events across North America to more than 35,000 people.

Equally important, I generated a six-figure income that allowed my wife to quit her job and join our business full-time. As my success grew, publishers began to court me with book contracts. I decided to trade-in my indie author hat and become a traditionally-published author. My self-published book was re-released with national distribution where it appeared in bookstores for over 10 years selling another 50,000 copies.

Did I ever hit any of the major bestseller lists? No, but I achieved something much more difficult. I discovered how to make a great living as an author through writing, speaking, and spin-off products.

My success, though, led to an unexpected path. Authors began to seek me out for marketing advice. I was happy to share what I had learned. But, the distress calls from struggling authors became so frequent that I saw there was a need for expert information about how to market books. This problem exists due to the lack of education that publishers provide to authors.

To meet the need for better marketing instruction, I started a consulting practice in 2007 called Wildfire Marketing. Since then, I've consulted with numerous publishers and coached over 600 fiction and non-fiction authors. My client list includes numerous *New York Times* bestsellers, such as Dr. Gary Chapman, Dr. John Townsend, Dr. Harville Hendrix, Lysa TerKeurst, DeVon Franklin, and Wanda Brunstetter. As new technology was developed, such as social media, online advertising, and the growth of Amazon, I studied how to use those digital tools to grow an author's book sales. I know what works and what is a waste of money.

As a consultant, I've helped first-time authors start out on the right foot. Plus, I've helped established authors achieve the highest levels of success. I also published my second book in 2012 with Writer's Digest called *Sell Your Book Like Wildfire*. However, since the publishing industry is constantly changing, I repackaged and self-published all of my marketing expertise into *The Author's Guides* series that you're reading now.

Today, I make a full-time living teaching authors and publishers how to sell more books. It's my dream job and I can't imagine doing anything else. Since I can't be everywhere at once, though, I wrote this book to multiply my efforts and help instruct and encourage as many authors as possible.

The reason why I share my background is because it's imperative that you take advice from someone who has achieved the same goal you seek. As the old adage says, "Never take financial advice from a broke person." Likewise, don't accept book marketing advice from someone who has never written a book or succeeded in selling their work. The publishing industry is filled with the "blind leading the blind." Instead, follow a leader who has gone before you, knows the difference between the landmines and shortcuts, and has the experience to help you navigate a successful path.

This book was written to serve as your personal guide to help you sell more books. In the coming pages, I will dispel a lot of myths and offer a lot of new ideas. However, the information will have no benefit unless you're willing to work at marketing your book. You cannot spend one hour a week on promotional activities and expect to grow. Neither should marketing be limited to only what you do when you're not writing. If you want to reach more readers, marketing should become synonymous with your writing. Engage in both activities throughout the course of your week and month.

I named my consulting practice Wildfire Marketing because I want to help you light a fire under your books, get them in front of more people, create a word-of-mouth wildfire, and enjoy the response of happy readers. When that happens, I hope you'll share your success story with me. That's the kind of tale that I like to read the most!

Rob Eagar

Wildfire Marketing

http://www.RobEagar.com

INTRODUCTION

Amazon is more than a website. It has become the most powerful book-selling machine ever invented. But, Amazon's power isn't reserved just for elite bestsellers. Their system was designed to help any author capture more sales.

Jeff Bezos founded the company in 1994 under the original name, "Cadabra," until a lawyer confused it with "cadaver." Another name, "Relentless," was also floated by Bezos, but people thought it sounded too sinister. (Fun fact: Type "Relentless.com" into your Internet browser and see where it goes.) The name "Amazon" was eventually chosen because it starts with the letter "A" and is the name of the world's largest river. Who would have thought the name would come to mean so much more?

Today, Amazon is the world's largest Internet retailer according to total revenue and one of the most valuable publicly-traded companies with a market capitalization over $1 trillion. That's a one with twelve zeros behind it!

More important to you and me, Amazon completely dominates the publishing industry. Take a moment to consider these mind-blowing statistics:

- Amazon sells close to 50% of all print books in America.
- Amazon sells over 70% of all e-books in America.
- Amazon is the largest sales account for almost every publisher in America.
- Amazon pays over 1,000 indie authors more than $100,000 in book royalties each year.
- Amazon's market share continues to increase both in America and around the world.

Sources:

http://authorearnings.com/report/february-2017/

http://authorearnings.com/report/dbw2017/

https://www.sec.gov/Archives/edgar/data/1018724/000119312518121161/d456916dex991.htm

Note: The term "indie author" in the list above refers to an independent author who self-publishes using Amazon's KDP service. These authors manage the writing, formatting, and marketing functions for their books but receive a royalty rate of 35% – 70%

Just like nothing can stop the Amazon River from flooding its banks in South America, nothing seems to stop Amazon from it ever-expanding efforts to sell more books. All the while, the only legitimate competition that exists, Barnes & Noble, continues to struggle with sluggish sales.

If the facts above don't get your attention, allow me to make things very clear:

Amazon sells more books than anyone else. Therefore, if you want to sell more books, you must learn how to sell more books through Amazon.

It doesn't matter if you're self-published or traditionally-published. It doesn't matter if you write fiction or non-fiction. It doesn't matter if you're a first-time author or an experienced bestseller. Success for every author hinges upon selling more books on Amazon.

That's why I wrote *The Author's Guide to Marketing Books on Amazon.* You need to know how to increase your book sales where it matters most...on Amazon. This no-nonsense guide takes the guesswork out of promoting your books on their website. You will learn how to:

- Boost sales with marketing text readers can't resist
- Identify categories that propel your book up the Amazon bestseller charts
- Secure influential customer reviews that convince readers to purchase
- Achieve maximum visibility for your book with low-cost Amazon ads
- Utilize little-known secrets within Author Central
- Grow your author email list for free using Amazon's massive audience

You can't control Amazon's dominance over the publishing industry. But, you can control the way your books appear on Amazon's website and entice more readers to purchase.

There are occasions throughout this book where I provide links to resources and companies that might be helpful. To be clear, I do not receive any commission or revenue from these links. They are just my recommendations for you to explore and decide if it's a good fit for your needs.

Before we begin, here's how I suggest using this book to get the best results:

- Read the entire book first to get the big picture.
- Don't try to do everything at once or you'll wind up overwhelmed.
- Do not compare yourself to other authors or you'll get depressed.
- Decide on one key priority to make your focus for the next 30 – 90 days.
- Experience a quick short-term result and build on that success.
- Don't expect overnight miracles. None of my *New York Times* bestselling clients attained success overnight. Each author worked for years to reach the highest level.

Let's get started. There is a lot of great information that I'm excited to share with you!

MASTER YOUR AMAZON BOOK DETAIL PAGE

Amazon may be the dominant bookseller around the world. However, there is a greater force that Amazon will never be able to dominate. That greater force is the power of language. If there is only one truth that every author needs to learn, it is this fact:

Language drives the book sale, not technology or companies.

People choose to buy books based upon the word of mouth they hear, the customer reviews they see, and the marketing copy they read. Technology and big companies merely deliver those words to our eyes and ears in more ways than ever before. Words sway people's minds, not computers.

I agree that Amazon's innovative technology revolutionized the publishing industry. Their one-click buy buttons, their invention of the Kindle e-reader, their automated book recommendation algorithms, and their customer review system are unparalleled. But, Amazon did not change the way books are sold. Their innovations simply made it easier for the way books were already being sold to occur at a faster pace. Amazon made it possible to put convincing language in front of a lot more readers.

Therefore, if you want to sell more books, start by creating superior marketing language. There is no better, faster, or cheaper way to persuade someone to buy your book than using powerful words. Best of all, great language doesn't cost anything to develop and gives more control over the way readers think, feel, and purchase.

However, too many authors mistakenly believe that technology is the primary driver of book sales. This idea is understandable considering how much technology affects our daily lives, including the Internet, social media, computers, and e-reader devices. But, we are not robots forced to buy books. People purchase books according to their free will.

Therefore, you can master technology and still fail at selling books. Millions of books were sold before the Internet existed. Amazon may have revolutionized the publishing industry by introducing new technology. But, Amazon's system is just a new means to the same end. The "end" is the ability to showcase words that convince readers to buy your book.

That's why this first chapter is dedicated to the power of language, specifically your book detail page on Amazon's website. The "book detail page" is where you have the opportunity to convert a reader's interest into a purchase.

Your book detail page is the place where people can see all of the details about your book, including the cover art, marketing text, author bio, and customer reviews.

If you display persuasive text, you can convince readers to click on the all-important "Add to Cart" button and purchase a copy. I want to help you maximize your book detail page to increase sales as much as possible.

First, let's make sure you understand the importance of Amazon's book detail page. As I mentioned in the Introduction, Amazon sells close to 50% of all print books and 70% of all e-books in the United States. If you want to increase your book sales, you would be wise to maximize your presence on Amazon. In other words, your book sales hinge upon the words and information that appear on your book detail page.

If you have an effective book detail page, it will help increase your sales. In contrast, if you have a boring book detail page, it can hinder your sales. Fortunately, there are already excellent book detail pages on Amazon's website that you can follow as examples.

Examples of Effective Book Detail Pages

Let's examine two stellar book detail pages on Amazon. The purpose of viewing these samples isn't to intimidate you or lead you to compare yourself to other authors. I just want to make sure you understand what an effective page looks like. Then, I'll explain how you can create standout text for your own book detail page.

For our fiction example, let's review a novel written by Paula Hawkins called *The Girl on the Train*. Use the link below if you'd like to view the actual book detail page on Amazon:

https://www.amazon.com/Girl-Train-Paula-Hawkins/dp/1594634025/

You might be familiar with this novel because it was turned in to a popular movie. When you view the book detail page for this title on Amazon, notice the descriptive text at the very top. Observe how the words grab your attention. The marketing text begins in a bolded font and hooks your interest by saying:

The #1 *New York Times* Bestseller, *USA Today* Book of the Year, now a major motion picture starring Emily Blunt.

The debut psychological thriller that will forever change the way you look at other people's lives, from the author of *Into the Water*.

"Nothing is more addicting than *The Girl on the Train*."—*Vanity Fair*

These initial sentences that describe *The Girl on the Train* are a great example of compelling marketing copy. Also, notice that when you see these lines on the Amazon page, there's a link that says, "Read more." If you click on that link, you'll see additional marketing text followed by a brief persuasive description of the plot.

The "Read more" link is important, because Amazon forces you to earn people's attention. On every book detail page, including the one for your book, you only get about 30 – 40 words of marketing copy to grab someone's interest. If you don't get people's attention with those first 30 – 40 words, few shoppers will click on the "Read more" link and see the rest of your marketing copy. *The Girl on the Train* is an excellent example of how to use language that propels people into learning more about your book. Let's examine why the words are so effective.

The first sentence mentions three major accolades that set the book apart from its competition. For example, it's a *New York Times* bestseller, *USA Today* Book of the Year, and the genesis for a major motion picture. If your book has received any type of major awards, put those achievements at the top of your book detail page.

In the second sentence, notice a clever trick that the publisher presented while describing the book. It says:

The debut psychological thriller that will forever change the way you look at other people's lives, from the author of *Into the Water*.

The end of that sentence says, "...from the author of *Into the Water*." Why is that clever? Those words help cross-promote another title by the same author. You may have never known that Paula Hawkins also wrote *Into the Water* if those words weren't displayed. But, the publisher made sure that you knew. Likewise, you can cross-promote your other books in a similar fashion using your marketing text.

After that sentence, the book detail page displays additional endorsements and a short, but powerful, description of the plot. My favorite part is how the marketing copy ends with a question that acts like a cliffhanger. Look at the concise synopsis below:

EVERY DAY THE SAME

Rachel takes the same commuter train every morning and night. Every day she rattles down the track, flashes past a stretch of cozy suburban homes, and stops at the signal that allows her to daily watch the same couple breakfasting on their deck. She's even started to feel like she knows them. Jess and Jason, she calls them. Their life—as she sees it—is perfect. Not unlike the life she recently lost.

UNTIL TODAY

And, then she sees something shocking. It's only a minute until the train moves on, but it's enough. Now everything's changed. Unable to keep it to herself, Rachel goes to the police. But is she really as unreliable as they say? Soon she is deeply entangled not only in the investigation but in the lives of everyone involved. Has she done more harm than good?

This description of *The Girl on the Train* is compelling. There's an emotional summary of the plot that leaves you with a suspenseful cliffhanger. But, it all starts with a list of industry awards and endorsements from major media. You can see why this book is an outstanding example of an effective book detail page on Amazon. The language captures a reader's interest and helps drive the book sale.

Let's change genres and look at a non-fiction example. I recommend the book detail page for *Getting Past No: Negotiating In Difficult Situations* by William Ury. Use the link below to view it on Amazon:

https://www.amazon.com/Getting-Past-Negotiating-Difficult-Situations/dp/0553371312/

This book detail page also starts with persuasive marketing text. The opening sentences aren't in a bolded font, and I would recommend making that text adjustment. But, the book description is quite powerful:

We all want to get to yes, but what happens when the other person keeps saying no?

How can you negotiate successfully with a stubborn boss, an irate customer, or a deceitful coworker?

In Getting Past No, William Ury of Harvard Law School's Program on Negotiation offers a proven breakthrough strategy for turning adversaries into negotiating partners. You'll learn how to:

- *Stay in control under pressure*
- *Defuse anger and hostility*
- *Find out what the other side really wants*
- *Counter dirty tricks*
- *Use power to bring the other side back to the table*
- *Reach agreements that satisfies both sides' needs*

Getting Past No is the state-of-the-art book on negotiation for the twenty-first century. It will help you deal with tough times, tough people, and tough negotiations. You don't have to get mad or get even. Instead, you can get what you want!

This book marketing text for *Getting Past No* may not display all of the industry awards and media endorsements as seen

for *The Girl on the Train*. But, the words are just as persuasive. Both books have achieved above average sales and
continue to sell a lot of copies years after being published.

Note: You may not know that any author can make changes
to their book detail page on Amazon at any time. For
instance, you can manually update your book description
with better copy or updated awards. Hold tight...I will
explain how to update your book detail page in Chapter 4 –
"Amazon's Secret Marketing Back Door."

What If You're Just Getting Started?

You might be a first-time author or a writer early in your
career. When you see the examples of *The Girl on the Train*
or *Getting Past No*, you might think, "Those are bestselling
books from established authors. I can't match their success.
How do I create a persuasive book detail page when I'm just
beginning my career with no accolades?" Fear not, there are
several steps any budding author can take:

1. List endorsements from notable leaders

When it comes to marketing language, nothing you say
about your book will ever be as powerful as what other
people say about your book. People tend to trust the
opinion of a peer more than the marketing text from an
advertisement. That's why you see so many books
displaying endorsements from notable leaders.

Examples of persuasive endorsements can be a recommendation from a well-known author who writes similar books

in your genre. Or, it could be a testimonial from a notable business executive, athlete, minister, musician, politician, etc.

If you know anyone famous, send them a free copy of your book and ask if they would provide you with an endorsement. If you don't know anyone famous, I bet you have a friend who knows someone famous. Ask your friend if they would make an introduction or pass along your book and facilitate an endorsement.

When I began my author career in 2002, no one had ever heard of me. I had to build my credibility by reaching out to other leaders and asking if they would endorse my book. It wasn't always an easy request to make. But, I was surprised by how many testimonials I received by politely asking. The key to my success was having the courage to persistently pursue endorsements. If you don't believe in your book, no one else will.

2. Display local or regional awards

Persuasive language can also include any local or regional awards that your book might have received. You may not have hit a major bestseller list. But, almost every area of the country offers regional literary contests and book awards. Most of these contests are either free or inexpensive to enter.

Do a little research on Google and search for local contests in your area where your book would qualify. You don't have to win the contest. If you get nominated within a specific category, add that mention to the top of your book detail page. For example, you could display, "Winner of the Southeast Regional Book Award" or "Nominated for Best New Fiction Writer of the Northwest." If you win a legitimate award, let the world know by listing it at the top of your book detail page.

3. Display "Over 100 Positive Reviews"

The amount of positive reviews your book receives on Amazon represents another type of influential language. Many Amazon shoppers judge books based on the positive and negative reviews from other readers. Therefore, once you receive at least 100 positive reviews, turn that achievement into an accolade featured at the top of your book detail page. Amazon defines any 5-star and 4-star review as positive. So, you can combine those two groups together into one total number.

By the way, if you are struggling to get more Amazon reviews, I will cover this topic next in Chapter 2 – "Four Ways to Get More Customer Reviews for Free."

You may not receive 100 positive reviews overnight. But, it's a realistic achievement for any author to pursue within a few months or a year. Once you reach that mark, add the achievement to the top of your book detail page. If you get 250, 500, or even 1,000 positive reviews, continue to update that number for people to see. Let the accomplishment act like social proof to convince other readers that your book is worth buying.

Your book may not yet be at the level of *The Girl on the Train* or *Getting Past No*. But, any author can take advantage of the three steps just described to display credible marketing text at the top of your book detail page.

Seven Elements of an Effective Book Detail Page

Now that you've seen excellent examples of book detail pages, let's walk through the seven key elements to make your page more effective on Amazon.

Book Detail Page Element #1 – The Marketing Hook

The most important element of any book detail page is a compelling marketing hook. You saw samples of great hooks for *The Girl on the Train* and *Getting Past No*. Your marketing hook is the first 30 – 40 words of promotional text that shoppers can see at the top of your book's page. This small amount of words is all that Amazon typically lets people see before having to click on a "Read more" link.

Amazon likes to maximize space on their book details pages, so they hide most of your book description text under a link that says, "Read more." If you can't get readers to click this link and read all of your marketing text, they probably aren't very interested in buying your book. They'll leave your book page and go look at another author's book. Therefore, the first 30 – 40 words that people see about your book are vital.

Also, Amazon's website is crowded with so much information that I recommend using bolded text to make your marketing hook stand out and grab people's attention.

In most cases, your marketing hook will be one or two sentences that generate curiosity about your book. However, a marketing hook can also include touting a major achievement that boosts your book's credibility, such as displaying a national bestseller award, a major sales milestone, or an endorsement from a famous person, high-profile media outlet, or a well-known organization.

If your book made it onto the *New York Times, USA Today, Wall Street Journal, Los Angeles Times,* or *Publishers Weekly* bestseller lists, display that achievement first. Those well-known names serve as an effective hook to capture a reader's attention. Telling people your book is a genuine bestseller attracts interest, because bestseller lists act like a form of word of mouth. Hitting a bestseller list means a lot of people thought a book was worth purchasing. All of their purchases act like a big group of people positively suggesting that other shoppers should consider buying the same book.

Additionally, if your book has crossed a major sales milestone, include that detail at the top of your book detail page. Typically, when you sell over 50,000 copies, 100,000 copies, 500,000 copies, and especially 1,000,000 units, those impressive achievements cause readers to take notice. Display that accomplishment as part of your marketing hook. Touting big sales is a good way to hook people's attention.

You may not have hit a bestseller list or sold 100,000 books, but you might have a major endorsement from a well-known leader, athlete, or celebrity. If so, put that testimonial at the top of your book detail page as a marketing hook for people to see.

For example, if you look up the book, *Factfulness*, by Hans Rosling on Amazon's website, you will see an endorsement at the top of the book detail page from Bill Gates. As the founder of Microsoft, Mr. Gates is so famous that many people will buy *Factfulness* based on his recommendation alone. His positive comments serves as a persuasive marketing hook. Use the link below to see his endorsement prominently displayed on the book detail page:

https://www.amazon.com/dp/1250107814

If you don't have a bestseller award, sales milestone, or a major endorsement, that's okay. Most books don't have these items. You have other options to display like I just addressed in the previous section, "What if . you're just getting started?"

Fortunately, every author can use the power of language to attract reader interest. If you don't have a fancy award or testimonial to exhibit, then create and show an attention-grabbing statement called a "book hook."

A "book hook" is a sentence or question designed to generate immediate curiosity that makes the reader desire to know more. A hook is meant to do one thing: get people's attention. It's nearly impossible to sell a book to someone who is distracted, dispassionate, or disinterested. To capture attention, create language that stops people in their tracks.

My favorite technique to develop a book hook is to start with the question, *"What if I told you...,"* and then fill in the blank. When you develop a hook using this question, it's easier for your brain to think of attention-grabbing words and phrases.

For instance, if you write fiction, think of the most suspenseful or emotional part of your story. Then, apply the *"What if I told you"* question to that scene. Notice how the technique worked to create an interesting hook for these popular novels that were turned into movies:

What if the first man to walk on Mars is sure he'll be the first to die there?

The Martian by Andy Weir

What if a high-end law firm is secretly a front for the Mafia?

The Firm by John Grisham

If you write non-fiction, create a hook by identifying the most counterintuitive parts of your manuscript or self-help instruction. Look for material where you say something that would make people think, "I've never heard that before..." or "I've never heard it put that way." Those types of counter-intuitive statements can be the seeds for an effective hook.

Apply the *"What if I told you"* question to your contrarian statements and let your creativity develop some thought-provoking options. For instance, notice how the following questions get your attention because they fly in the face of accepted beliefs:

What if you could be debt-free in 12 months, no matter how much you owe?

What if overcoming harmful habits has nothing to do with self-control?

What if trying to make everyone happy only makes you feel worse?

These questions grab your attention. That's the purpose of a hook. And, you can drop the "what if" portion of the question and create a short, punchy statement, such as:

Be debt-free in 12 months - no matter how much you owe.

If you've never created a marketing hook before, the process may feel difficult at first. For detailed help, read my book, *The Author's Guide to Write Text That Sells Books.* This resource breaks down the process using a step-by-step formula that any fiction or non-fiction author can follow.

When shoppers visit your book detail page on Amazon, your goal is to grab their attention with a hook using the first 30 - 40 words. Your hook might be an accolade, an endorsement, or a clever statement. But, you must display your hook at the top in order to get the best results. Once you arrest people's attention, then you're ready to move to the second element of the process.

Book Detail Page Element #2 – The Book Description

The next key element of your book detail page is the book description, also known as the "back cover copy." That's because publishers usually take the words created for a book's back cover and put the same text on the book's Amazon page.

I recommend using different approaches to write descriptions for a non-fiction book versus a fiction novel. If you're new to writing a description for your book, use the following templates as a guide to aid the process.

Write a Nonfiction Book Description in 5 Easy Steps

In order for a nonfiction book description to be successful, create marketing language that resonates with readers in these ways:

- Understand how the reader feels
- Understand what the reader wants

When people consider buying a nonfiction book, they are usually motivated by an internal desire to solve a problem, learn something new, or feel more inspired. However, logic makes people think, but emotion makes them act. When you identify the underlying feeling that is motivating the reader, then you create an emotional connection that makes the reader think, "This author understands me."

When readers believe that you understand how they feel, they become more open to the solution offered within your book. This opens the door to explain how you understand what they want, which is the desired payoff that makes your book worth purchasing.

In its simplest form, your book description is meant to show readers that you understand how they feel and recognize what they want. To address these two goals, use the following five-step template to walk through the process. I'll describe each step of the template first. Then, I'll apply the template to the book description for *Getting Past No*, so that you can see the five steps in action.

Step 1 – Start with a marketing hook

Always start your book description with a marketing hook. Make it stand out as a separate sentence from the rest of your text. As I emphasized in the previous section, you must get people's attention in the first 30 - 40 words before you can tell them anything else about your book. If you fail to get the reader's attention, the next four steps of writing your book description can be wasted.

Step 2 – Tell the reader you know how they feel

In the second step, tell the reader that you understand how they feel. In most cases, you wrote your non-fiction book to address a problem or a felt need that people want to resolve. State how you understand that problem or felt need in 1 – 2 sentences. This step allows people to recognize why your book is worth considering. To show people you know what they are feeling, use these fill-in-the-blank phrases as idea starters, such as:

Are you tired of _____?

Do you wish you could ____?

Do you love ___, but hate ___?

The number one problem today is _____.

You want _____, but instead _____ happens.

Step 3 – Tell the reader you know what they want

Once readers agree that you know how they feel, they become emotionally open to the payoff your book can provide. Thus, the third step is to explain the value and results offered by your book. You are essentially explaining that you know what the reader wants. Use these questions and phrases below to spark ideas:

My book will help you _____.

How will your book specifically improve the reader's condition?

How will your book educate or inspire the reader?

What specific results will readers experience from applying your book to their lives?

In most cases, it's wise to display the payoff from your book as a list of bulleted statements that readers can easily see. Each bullet point on your list should explain a specific type of value that the reader will receive. You'll see good examples in the next section when we apply this template to *Getting Past No.*

If you're new to the concept of writing marketing text that explains the results offered by your book, I recommend reading Chapter 3 - "Explain Your Book Payoff With Value Statements," in my book, *The Author's Guide to Write Text That Sells Books.* You want the payoff from your book to be easily understood by readers. If they miss seeing the payoff, you can miss the book sale.

Step 4 – Tell the reader you can be trusted

The fourth step is meant to address skepticism that can linger in people's minds if they have never heard of you or your book. Many readers can wonder, "Can I trust this author with my time and money?" If they remain uncertain, their skepticism can cost you the book sale. So, the next step in this template is to minimize doubt by describing your credibility and showing readers that they can trust you. For example, you could mention the following credentials:

- Professional certifications, such as Ph.D., CPA, AIA, M.D., LMFT, etc.
- Professional or industry awards, such as Who's Who, Top 30 under 30, etc.
- Job title, such as President, Founder, Professor, Vice President, Director, etc.
- Past experience, such as 5, 10, or 25 years working in a particular field
- Bestselling author of _____
- Author whose books have sold over 50,000, 100,000, or 1 million copies.
- Local or regional awards, such as Winner of the Texas Writer's Book Award

People won't know about your experience and credentials unless you display them. You don't have to be a Ph.D. to convince readers, just give enough information to build trust.

Step 5 – End with a Call to Action

A persuasive book description should finish with a bang, rather than a whimper. Tell the reader to buy your book.

You may think this step is a crass or unnecessary, but nothing could be further from the truth. Never forget how easy it is for a shopper on Amazon to leave your book page and buy a different book instead.

When you have the reader's attention, don't trip at the finish line. Use this last step to close the sale by telling the reader to purchase. It doesn't mean you're insulting their intelligence. Instead, you are reinforcing the idea that buying your book is a good choice that shouldn't be delayed. Feel free to use language that fits your personality. But, display some type of call to action for people to see. Otherwise, you will miss out on extra sales that you could easily close. For example, use phrases like these below to prompt the reader:

Buy your copy today.

Enjoy reading "insert your title."

Get it now.

Experience these results today.

Learn how today.

Buy a copy of "insert your title."

When you put the five steps of the template together, you have a complete process to write an effective book description:

Step 1 – Start with a marketing hook

Step 2 – Tell the reader you know how they feel

Step 3 – Tell the reader you know what they want

Step 4 – Tell the reader you can be trusted

Step 5 – Give a call to action

To see these steps in action, observe how they appear in the book description for *Getting Past No*. For example, the description starts with an effective Step 1 marketing hook:

We all want to get to yes, but what happens when the other person keeps saying no?

This question works as a marketing hook, because any reader who wants to improve their negotiation skills will see those words and think, "Yes, I keep getting confounded when people tell me no. Okay, you've got my attention."

Next, the book description moves to Step 2 by specifically describing issues the reader is feeling:

How can you negotiate with a stubborn boss, an irate customer, or a deceitful co-worker?

Almost everyone can relate to the frustrating experiences described in that question. So, the reader thinks, "This author understands what I feel."

The next part of this book description reverses Steps 3 and 4, which still works effectively. Since William Ury has an impressive bio teaching at Harvard University, his credibility based on Step 4 is moved earlier in the book description and validated by the next sentence:

William Ury of Harvard Law School's Program on Negotiation offers a proven breakthrough strategy for turning adversaries into negotiating partners.

Lastly, the book description concludes by explaining how the author understands what the reader wants. This step presents an excellent list of bullet points and a closing paragraph that specifically describes the payoff for the reader. Plus, the last sentence covers Step 5, which displays a persuasive call to action:

You will learn how to:

- *Stay in control under pressure*
- *Defuse anger and hostility*
- *Find out what the other side really wants*
- *Counter dirty tricks*
- *Use power to bring the other side back to the table*
- *Reach agreements that satisfies both sides' needs*

Getting Past No is the state-of-the-art book on negotiation for the twenty-first century. It will help you deal with tough times, tough people, and tough negotiations. You don't have to get mad or get even. Instead, you can get what you want!

If the reader desires to improve their negotiation skills, you can see how this book description presents a potent reason to buy a copy.

If you write nonfiction, especially educational or self-help content, use this five-step template as an easy guide to follow. Start with an attention-grabbing hook, describe the felt need, explain the exciting payoff, define your author credibility, and close with a call to action.

Write a Fiction Book Description in 3 Easy Steps

If you write novels, you can create a persuasive book description or "synopsis" using this three-step template. I'll weave the marketing text from our earlier example, *The Girl on the Train*, to show how the steps work together.

Step 1 – Display your book hook

Step 2 – Describe your main character in conflict

Step 3 – Close with a cliffhanger

Step 1 – Display your book hook

Every book description, including fiction, should start with a captivating hook. Otherwise, how will you grab people's attention? To create a marketing hook for a novel, think like a screenwriter trying to pitch your story as a movie using just one sentence. Or, use the *"What if I told you"* technique described earlier in this chapter.

If we use *The Girl on the Train* as an example, the initial marketing hook that people see on Amazon are all of the amazing accolades. But, before the book won those awards, this is the one sentence hook that readers would see:

EVERY DAY THE SAME...UNTIL TODAY.

I appreciate the simplicity of this short sentence and the power of presenting the words in all caps on the book's Amazon page, which is optional. If you review the book description for *The Girl on the Train* on Amazon, you may notice the hook sentence is split over two paragraphs to add a visual effect. This approach is also optional. As long as readers can clearly see the arresting hook, then you can grab people's attention.

Step 2 – Describe your main character in conflict

After displaying your hook in Step 1, the next step is to describe your main character experiencing intense conflict. Almost every genre of fiction involves a story where the protagonist is thrown into an extreme level of strife, confusion, or danger. The settings may be different, the hero and villain personalities may be diverse, but every great story revolves around the main character trying to resolve conflict and achieve a goal. It is the conflict that attracts the reader's interest.

Therefore, it is your goal in Step 2 to describe emotional conflict to the point where the reader can also feel it. In other words, it is not your goal to explain the whole story or give a boring overview of your setting and all the characters involved. Keep this point in mind:

Don't tell people about the story. Tell people about the conflict.

If your synopsis doesn't make readers feel the conflict, then your description is too bland. Logic makes people think, but emotion makes them act. If you want more readers to buy your novel, make them feel the emotional angst. In fact, show your synopsis to a few friends and ask them if they feel anything when they read it. If not, you've got a dead synopsis. Start over and crank up the conflict even more.

You can develop emotional conflict for your synopsis from multiple places in your story. In many cases, you can describe the turmoil that the main character experiences in the opening scene. For example, the synopsis of *The Girl on the Train* opens with some basic information about the setting and the protagonist, Rachel. But, the description quickly moves to the turmoil that unfolds after she sees something shocking in the beginning of the story:

Rachel takes the same commuter train every morning and night. Every day she rattles down the track, flashes past a stretch of cozy suburban homes, and stops at the signal that allows her to daily watch the same couple breakfasting on their deck. She's even started to feel like she knows them. Jess and Jason, she calls them. Their life—as she sees it—is perfect. Not unlike the life she recently lost.

And, then she sees something shocking. It's only a minute until the train moves on, but it's enough. Now everything's changed. Unable to keep it to herself, Rachel goes to the police.

Most novelists are smart to plunge the protagonist into major conflict right away, because that's what draws the reader into the story. Thus, describe the conflict from your opening section for Step 2 of your synopsis.

However, there may be cases where the most intense conflict occurs in the middle or end of the story. That may be a good option. But, if you choose to pull conflict from those latter sections, be careful in your description to avoid giving away clues that could spoil the conclusion.

Whether you write romantic beach reads, cozy mysteries,

action thrillers, or gory horror stories, your goal is to weave dramatic conflict into your book description. Once the reader can feel the turmoil of the protagonist, then you're ready to close the sale with Step 3.

Step 3 – Close with a cliffhanger

Every reader knows that a novel is completely scripted by the author. But, if you tease readers properly, they will gladly pay money to find out what happens. That's the purpose of Step 3. Tease readers to the point where they must find out the ending.

You achieve this goal by writing a cliffhanger question or sentence that leaves the reader hanging on the edge of their seat.

Will the protagonist find true love?

Will the villain be stopped?

Will justice be served?

Now he's mad and it's payback time.

He broke her dreams. Now she's going to break his heart.

Always close your synopsis with a cliffhanger. This step is vitally important. Lead the reader to wonder what will happen next. For example, the description of *The Girl on the Train* ends with a provocative question:

But is Rachel really as unreliable as they say? Soon she is deeply entangled not only in the investigation but in the lives of everyone involved. Has she done more harm than good?

That's what I call a cliffhanger ending. If you enjoy reading suspense, you're hooked. You want to find out what happens.

A good cliffhanger can also serve as the "call to action," similar to Step 5 that I mentioned earlier in my nonfiction template. But, it can be wise to include a straightforward call to action at the end of your description that capitalizes on the reader's interest, such as:

Buy a copy today and find out what happens.

Get your copy today.

Purchase "insert your title" and find out what happens next.

Buy "insert your title" now.

Whether you're a budding novelist or a veteran bestseller, this three-step template can work for your synopsis. Grab the reader's attention with a hook, describe the main character in conflict, then close with a cliffhanger and call to action.

Are there other ways to create a great book description? Of course. I'm not here to tell you that there is only one way. You may develop a completely different approach that motivates readers to purchase. If it works, go with it.

But, if you've never written a book description, or if you feel stuck in a rut writing descriptive copy, use these templates as a guide to rekindle your creative juices.

. . .

Book Detail Page Element #3 – Endorsements

Let's revisit the idea of endorsements and assume you've secured a few testimonials from a well-known leader, athlete, celebrity, or musician. You may also receive a positive review from a highly-regarded magazine, newspaper, or blogger. The top of your book detail page on Amazon is the place to let those endorsements shine. Powerful testimonials act as attention-grabbing text to boost your author credibility.

However, if you have more than two high-profile endorsements, you can add the rest to your book detail page in one of two places:

1. List testimonials underneath your book description text as reinforcing commentary. Just remember that people won't see these endorsements unless they click on the "Read more" link to see your entire book description.

2. List your testimonials in a separate section further down your book detail page called "Editorial Reviews." This section is an area reserved by Amazon for publishers and authors to add endorsements from well-known influencers and media outlets. Authors can access this section of the page via Amazon's secret marketing "back door" that I discuss in Chapter 4.

When it comes to endorsements, keep in mind that people care more about who makes the comment, rather than the comment they make. Thus, you don't need to show a long, detailed testimonial. Just show the best parts of a person's testimonial and highlight their name for readers to see. It's the name that acts as the persuasive text.

Here's a little industry secret. Many of the testimonials that you see for other books were written by the author or the publisher first, then sent to the endorser for final approval. Most leaders are so busy that they don't have time to write an endorsement. But, they are more likely to approve a testimonial written for them that resembles their voice and personality.

If you want to get a busy leader to consider providing an endorsement for your book, offer to write the comment and send to them for review. Sometimes, you'll get a faster response using that time-saving technique.

I like to practice what I preach, so here's an example of how I display endorsements on my Amazon book page. Visit the link for my book, *Mastering Book Hooks For Authors*:

https://www.amazon.com/dp/B078L2FSFH

Scroll down below the book description where it says Editorial Reviews. You will see endorsements from several *New York Times* bestselling authors who are my past clients:

"I recommend Rob Eagar to any author looking to take their book campaign to a higher level."

Dr. Gary Chapman - #1 *New York Times* bestselling author of *The Five Love Languages*

"I give Rob Eagar my highest recommendation. If you want to increase book sales, make him the first person you hire."

Lysa TerKeurst - 4-time *New York Times* bestselling author

"Rob Eagar gets great results and strategically places authors in the right spaces. I'm happy with what Rob did for me, and I highly recommend him."

Dr. John Townsend - *New York Times* bestselling author of *Boundaries*

Like many authors, you probably see these endorsements and think, "Wow, Rob has worked with a lot of well-known authors who've been successful." Those testimonials boost my credibility with authors who would be interested to read my books or hire me as a consultant to grow their book sales.

Likewise, use endorsements to enhance your credibility with readers who are unfamiliar with your work. There is nothing you can say about yourself that is as powerful as what others say about you.

Book Detail Page Element #4 – Author Bio

The fourth element of your book detail page is your author bio. Earlier in this chapter, I talked about the importance of adding author credibility to a non-fiction book description. But, you also want readers to see your complete author bio if they'd like more details about you and your books.

If you have an Author Page set up on Amazon's website, their system will automatically insert that text onto your book detail page. You can create an Author Page by setting up a free Author Central Account (see Chapter 3 for details).

The Amazon Author Central Account allows you to upload one bio that will appear on all of your book detail pages. If you self-publish through the Amazon Kindle Direct Publishing (KDP) platform, you can adjust your bio through their system as well.

Ideally, you want your bio text to enhance your credibility. Avoid merely summarizing your books, bragging about your education, and running through a list of hobbies. No one really cares. Instead, use your author bio to describe how you've had a history of entertaining people (fiction) or helping people (non-fiction).

One way to improve your author bio is to read good examples from other authors already on Amazon. I've found the bios for Lisa Wingate and John Grisham to be better than average because they blend a mix of accolades with showing a desire to help other people. Use the links below to read their bios on Amazon:

Lisa Wingate (inspirational novelist)

https://www.amazon.com/Lisa-Wingate/e/B001HCX5WK/

John Grisham (legal thrillers)

https://www.amazon.com/John-Grisham/e/B000AQ40M8/

Book Detail Page Element #5 – Amazon Categories

The fifth element of your book detail page is a topic that can generate a lot of confusion among authors. This confusion is related to the Amazon categories selected for your book. On your book detail page, you will see your book's category information listed under the "Product details" section where the format, publisher, and ISBN number are displayed. At the bottom of this section, you will see a listing that says, "Amazon Best Sellers Rank." Below that phrase, there are three lines with different genre categories related to your book.

The Amazon Best Seller categories act like an online version of the bookshelves within a physical bookstore. For example, if you walk into a typical bookstore, you will see books arranged on shelves in different sections, such as history, business books, cookbooks, etc. The separate sections make it easy for customers to find the type of book that they want to buy by displaying the genre and specific topic.

Likewise, Amazon organizes the books they sell on their website by genre categories. However, their categories are more detailed than a physical bookstore. Amazon has thousands of genre categories and sub-categories. Many would be considered obscure, such as "Children's Pig Books," "Self-Esteem Skills," or novels classified as "Vigilante Justice." By organizing books according to unique categories, people can search Amazon's website for the exact type of book they want to read.

How do the Amazon's Best Seller categories affect you as an author? The categories act like beacons to help the right type of readers find your book within Amazon's huge inventory. It's like having your book displayed on the correct shelf in a bookstore. If you write political thrillers, you don't want your novel sitting on the cookbook shelf. The wrong type of reader would see your book and ignore it.

There's an art and science to choosing the right categories for your book. If you're traditionally-published, your publisher will select the categories for you and submit that information to Amazon's system. However, it's crucial to educate yourself on this process. In many cases, your publisher will choose categories that are too broad or even incorrect for your genre. If you're unaware of those mistakes, it can cost you a lot of lost book sales by preventing the right readers from seeing your book. Selecting the proper categories for your books is one of the easiest ways to get more marketing exposure on Amazon for free.

At the time of this writing, Amazon allows publishers to select five different categories for each book title. Authors who self-publish using Amazon's KDP service are allowed to select two categories for their books at the time of publication.

But, here's a clever trick. You can contact Amazon via your Author Central Account and ask them to manually add extra categories for your book. In fact, authors who self-publish through KDP (Kindle Direct Publishing) can add up to 10 total categories for a book. For details on this technique, see "Chapter 3 – Maximize Your Author Central Account."

Each book category on Amazon's website has a Top 100 list associated with that category. Many shoppers click on these

Top 100 lists to discover other books within a preferred category that they might want to read. Here's an example of how the Top 100 lists work for a book. Let's go back to the novel we discussed earlier, *The Girl on the Train*. Click on the link below to see the category information on Amazon's website:

https://www.amazon.com/Girl-Train-Paula-Hawkins/dp/1594634025/

At the time of this writing, the three Amazon book categories listed for the paperback version of *The Girl on the Train* appear as follows:

Books > Literature & Fiction > Literary

Books > Mystery, Thriller & Suspense > Thrillers & Suspense > Suspense

Books > Romance > Contemporary

Each of the category words and phrases listed above are hyperlinked to a page on Amazon's website that lists the Top 100 books within that category. If you click on any of these words, you will be taken to a new webpage that shows a Top 100 list for the bestselling books in that specific category. In other words, Amazon allows shoppers to easily see the other books people are buying within a specific genre. Therefore, choosing the right categories for your book is important for three reasons:

1. Selecting the right categories enables Amazon's algorithms to place your book in front of the right readers when they search the website.

2. Selecting the right categories helps your book appear in front of avid readers who browse the Top 100 lists looking for new book ideas.

3. Selecting the right categories helps your book qualify for free promotions to millions of targeted readers via Amazon's "bestseller badges" and daily email blasts.

Did you know that Amazon sends out thousands, possibly millions, of targeted email blasts every day to their customers? These emails contain curated promotions for books that customers might like. But, they also curate the top bestselling books from different Top 100 category lists. In essence, if your book appears on any of the most popular Top 100 Amazon lists, Amazon will do some free marketing for you. Imagine thousands of people receiving an email from Amazon that recommends your book.

To be candid, this process typically rewards the books that are already big bestsellers. So, it's a bit like the rich getting richer. Your book must be selling really well to qualify for the daily email blasts. But, if you or your publisher neglect to select the right categories for your book, then you'll never qualify in the first place. That's why choosing the appropriate category is an essential part of your book detail page.

When I teach authors how to select the best Amazon categories for their books, here are two tips that I recommend:

1. Start by choosing one broad category that's directly related to your book's primary content in order to get accurately cataloged within Amazon's overall inventory. This broad category will contain a lot more competition, but it's

vital for Amazon to know the right genre for your book. For example, if you write legal thrillers, choose the broad category: "Mystery, Thriller & Suspense."

2. Next, choose several narrow sub-categories with less potential competition. By selecting categories with less competition, you improve the odds of your book appearing on an Amazon Top 100 list. Doing so enables Amazon to help market your book to serial readers who browse those popular lists looking for new books to read.

For example, if you research and drill down into the broad Amazon book category of "Mystery, Thriller, & Suspense," you can find numerous sub-categories that could be good options to select with less competition, such as:

Crime fiction – Noir

Cozy mystery

Hard-boiled mystery

Serial killer

Men's adventure fiction

Selecting both broad and narrow categories works in conjunction to do two things simultaneously. First, you accurately place your book in Amazon's database using the broad category. Second, you enable Amazon's algorithms to help your book get more exposure by appearing in smaller sub-categories with less competition.

Your goal should be to keep your book on at least one or more Top 100 lists at all times. When your book makes it onto a Top 100 list, it receives the opportunity to be found by more readers on Amazon. Even better, if you reach #1 on a Top 100 list, then Amazon will add a bright orange "#1 Best Seller" badge to your book's detail page and any search results listings. When readers see that influential badge associated with your book, it helps close more sales.

In case you're wondering, Amazon doesn't make a complete listing of all their book categories available to the public. Instead, you have to do the research on your own. But, the process is easy and only takes an hour of research to yield plenty of good options.

Use this simple trick. Click on the category links for your own book (along with your book's competition) and go to the screen that displays the Top 100 bestseller lists. On the left side of the screen, you'll see a long list of related categories along with the broad "parent" category listed at the top. Click on each of the subcategories, go the Top 100 list, and check the Amazon sales ranking for the #1 bestselling book and #20 bestselling book. If your book maintains a sales ranking that is equal or better than those books, then you know that subcategory is a good candidate for your book. By placing your book into that category, you stand to get extra marketing exposure for free by appearing on that Top 100 bestseller list.

Continue to click on the various subcategories to see where the competition is weak. Also, click on the "parent" category at the top and drill down into other subcategories that relate to your genre.

Authors who self-publish using Amazon's KDP service are

able to select two categories when they initially upload their book manuscript. But, after the book is launched, you can contact Amazon's customer service team and add up to 10 total categories for a book. Adding more categories, especially sub-categories with little competition, is an easy way to help your book gain more sales for free. (See Chapter 3 for details about contacting Amazon to add more categories for your book).

NOTE: Amazon displays different category listings for paperbacks than they do for ebooks. So, be sure to monitor and adjust the categories for each version separately.

If you're a traditionally-published author or self-published a book using a third-party company other than Amazon, the category selection for your book is controlled by your publisher. Thus, before you turn in your final manuscript, do some research on the best categories for your book. Recommend those choices to your publisher to make sure Amazon's system is optimized to help promote your book.

Book Detail Page Element #6 – Customer Reviews

The sixth element of your book detail page relates to the customer reviews. This element causes some authors to shudder with fear and awe. That's because customer reviews are the most important factor for many Amazon shoppers when deciding to buy a book. The reviews they see can make or break the book sale.

Readers who check customer reviews on Amazon are like travelers using Tripadvisor before booking a hotel or foodies using Yelp before deciding on a good restaurant. The comments and the total amount of reviews that a book receives can play a major role in swaying a reader's decision.

Your primary goal is to get as many reviews as possible, even if some reviews are negative. That's because most readers are more influenced by the total number of reviews they see. A lot of reviews signals that a lot of other people have already found a book interesting.

You might be thinking, "How do I get a lot of customer reviews if I'm just getting started?" I'm here to help. Chapter 2 – "Four Ways to Get More Customer Reviews for Free" is dedicated to teaching you how to get more reviews, ethically and inexpensively.

Book Detail Page Element #7 – Cover Art

The seventh element is last in our discussion, but it appears first on your book detail page: the cover art for your book. The way your book cover appears on Amazon has a direct influence on your sales.

For instance, a self-published novelist came to me for marketing help because his sales were stagnant. The first problem I noticed was that his book covers looked home-made. We had a frank conversation where I told him the truth. At first, he resisted my advice and complained to his wife about my candid comments. But, she confessed to not liking his book covers either, which got his attention.

Fortunately, the author followed my guidance and hired a

professional designer to create amazing new covers. After uploading his new artwork to Amazon, the amount of books he sold per day doubled!

If your book sales aren't meeting expectations, take an objective look at your cover and compare it to the best-selling titles within your genre. If your cover appears subpar, I can guarantee that you're losing readers. Upgrade a bad-looking cover. This one step alone can be the fastest path to capturing more readers.

If your budget is tight, there are numerous ways to hire a professional graphic artist for less than $250 to design a cover. If you don't know a good designer, check out these websites to hire an inexpensive freelancer:

https://Reedsy.com

https://www.Upwork.com

https://www.Fiverr.com

If you want to sell more books on Amazon, display cover art and marketing text on your book detail page that persuades readers to purchase. In review, the seven elements of an effective book detail page include:

1. Marketing hook
2. Book description
3. Endorsements
4. Author bio

5. Amazon categories
6. Customer reviews
7. Cover art

I'll close this chapter with comforting news. You have complete control to improve each of these elements on your book detail page. However, ignoring these elements or taking a lackadaisical approach could cost you a lot of lost book sales over time. Take the initiative to maximize the way your book appears on Amazon. If you utilize the power of language correctly, you will persuade more readers to buy your book.

After reading this chapter, you may suddenly feel compelled to address problems with your book detail page. But, how do you access Amazon's website to make better language appear to readers? Most authors think only their publisher can make changes to a book's Amazon detail page. That's not true.

Here's a little secret. It doesn't matter if you're an indie author or a traditionally-published author. Anyone can access their book detail page and make changes whenever they want. I will reveal this covert technique in Chapter 4 – "How to Access Amazon's Secret Marketing Back Door."

If you're dying to know this secret now, jump ahead to Chapter 4. Otherwise, the next chapter will explain several ways to get more Amazon customer reviews for free!

2

FOUR WAYS TO GET CUSTOMER REVIEWS FOR FREE

Put yourself in the position of a shopper on Amazon who is looking for a new novel to read. Let's say you're someone who really likes mystery and suspense. You've got some time to kill (pardon the pun), and you'd like a good book to read.

You go to Amazon's website and browse for books in the mystery genre. As you search Amazon's website, you come across a book called, *The Plea*, which has 59 customer reviews listed. All of the reviews are mostly positive.

However, as you continue searching on Amazon, you see another book called, *A Criminal Defense* that has over 7,100 customer reviews. Most of those reviews are also positive. Everything else being equal, which book would you buy?

Based on the fact that one book has over 7,000 reviews, you'd probably select *A Criminal Defense*. Indeed, most Amazon shoppers made that decision as well. At the time of this writing, both books were originally published around the same date. Yet, the sales for *A Criminal Defense* outpaced *The Plea* by a wide margin according to the Amazon's sales rankings.

Are customer reviews really that much of a difference maker? Absolutely. Here's the reason why:

Nothing attracts a crowd like a crowd.

When a book has a lot of Amazon reviews, it communicates to other readers that there is a lot of interest in that title. The reviews appear like an online crowd who has gathered to have a large, lively conversation about that book. Other readers who see this "crowd" are drawn to find out what's happening.

They see a lot of activity, a lot of discussion, and some people arguing various opinions. When shoppers see that type of online activity on Amazon, they are drawn to the book and think, "This looks like an interesting choice that I might want to purchase."

For instance, have you ever come upon a crowd unexpectedly, felt yourself grow curious, and then asked someone nearby, "What's going on?" As humans, we are naturally drawn to crowds. The same dynamic occurs on Amazon when a book accrues a lot of customer reviews.

How many reviews does it take to create an online crowd? I recommend setting a goal to attract at least 100 reviews as fast as possible. Once you cross the 100-review threshold, that's usually enough activity to signal that a lot of people have been talking about your book.

If you're a first-time author, you may consider that number and think, "Wow, 100 reviews! How will ever get that many?" Trust me, if you write a good book, remain patient, and use the techniques that I describe, you will reach and eventually surpass that goal. The more reviews your book receives, the more your book becomes attractive to new readers. It's the process of success breeding more success.

Obviously, the best way to get more customer reviews is to write an amazing book. Shoddy work will generally produce a lack of interest and a lack of reviews. However, there are steps that any author can take to be proactive and attract more reviews.

In this chapter, I will explain four ways you can get more Amazon customer reviews for free. Everybody loves the word, "free." So, I'm going to show you how to do it without spending any money. Once you see these tactics, you'd be crazy not to implement them for your books.

The Ethics of Customer Reviews

Before we dive into specifics, let's address three emotional issues that concern authors regarding customer reviews.

First, let's talk about ethical behavior. When some authors realize the importance of getting more Amazon reviews, they feel tempted to act unethically and pursue options that are shady. For example, there are online services that will offer to write reviews for your book for a fee and others that specialize in creating a bunch of fake reviews.

Hear me clearly. Never pay anyone to get more customer

reviews. Don't try to fake it. Don't do anything unethical. Not only can your author reputation be ruined, but you and your book can be blacklisted by Amazon. Imagine getting kicked off of Amazon's website altogether. It's not worth the risk to do something stupid, especially when there are several ways to get more reviews properly and maintain your dignity.

Second, never bribe people to write a review for your book. According to Amazon's guidelines:

You may provide free or discounted copies of your books to readers. However, you may not demand a review in exchange or attempt to influence the review. Offering anything other than a free or discounted copy of the book—including gift cards—will invalidate a review, and we'll have to remove it.

Source: https://kdp.amazon.com/en_US/help/ topic/G202101910

If you offer people tangible gifts or compensation to write a review, then you'll be in violation of Amazon's policies. Don't do it. It's not worth losing your reputation over getting a few extra reviews. However, in my opinion, it is okay to offer people intangible, non-monetary appreciation for writing a review, such as offering access to a personal Q&A session with the author.

For example, I've told the members of my book launch team that anyone who writes a review would receive access to a personal webinar where I would take their questions. This form of gratitude encourages people to write reviews without violating Amazon's policies.

Third, some authors are terrified of receiving negative reviews. Any unflattering comment on Amazon causes them to curl up in the fetal position and weep. This anxiety is based on a misconception. In reality, negative reviews are actually a good thing, because they help provide a genuine dialogue about your book. If every review was 5-star, many savvy shoppers would feel concerned that people weren't speaking the truth. No book is perfect, and neither is yours.

Accept a few negative reviews and don't obsess over them. See them as a positive asset to the overall conversation around your book. But, if you get a lot of negative reviews, that's another story. In that case, you may need to accept the constructive criticism and improve your writing skills where the criticism is valid.

On the other hand, if you receive an abusive or slanderous review, you don't have to take it lying down. You can ask Amazon to remove any review that is deemed abusive, such as someone criticizing your character or reputation. I'll show how to report abusive reviews to Amazon in Chapter 3. For now, let's use this chapter to secure more positive reviews from readers without spending a dime.

Who is Eligible to Post a Customer Review?

There is a mistaken belief that only readers who bought your book on Amazon can post a customer review. For example, you might see the tag, "Verified Purchase," next to a lot of reviews on their website. This tag has led some authors to believe that non-Amazon customers aren't able to post a review. That is not true.

People can buy your book from a different retailer, get a copy from the library, or receive an advance reader copy, and still qualify to post a review. That's why you will see some reviews on Amazon with the "Verified Purchase" tag and some reviews without that tag.

At the time of this writing, Amazon's eligibility requirement for posting reviews is listed on their website as follows:

To contribute to Customer Reviews, you must have spent at least $50 on Amazon.com using a valid credit or debit card in the past 12 months.

Source: https://www.amazon.com/gp/help/customer/display.html?nodeId=201929730

According to Amazon, anyone who spends $50 buying books or other products on their website can qualify to write a book review for the next 12 months. Naturally, it makes sense that people should only post a review if they've read the book. But, they don't have to buy the book on Amazon. This means you can ask people to write a review even if they purchased your book somewhere else or received it as a gift.

Four Methods to Get Customer Reviews for Free

Let's move past the ethical concerns to discuss the good stuff. How do you attract more reviews to your book for free? Employ these four steps:

1. Reach out to email subscribers and social media fans

The easiest way to get a lot of customer reviews quickly is to reach out to two groups of friendly people: your email subscribers and social media followers.

If you aren't familiar with the importance of building an author email list, I encourage you to read, *The Author's Guide to Email Marketing*, by yours truly. Email is the best way for any author to sell more books of any genre. It's proven to be 12 times better at generating e-commerce sales than all social media combined. Plus, there is a side benefit to building an email list. You assemble a group of fans who can be willing to help you out with other marketing activities, such as writing Amazon reviews for your book.

In addition, you can make a similar request of your friends on social media. They also comprise a group of digital fans who can participate in activities to help market your book. If you use a variety of platforms, such as Facebook, Instagram, Twitter, or LinkedIn, send your review request to each separate group.

When you ask your fans to write a review, encourage people to take action if they have already purchased your book. Buying your book on Amazon isn't a requirement for readers to write a review, but it does help prevent any concerns about unethical activity from Amazon's perspective.

Of course, not everyone will respond to your request, but certainly no one will respond if you don't ask in the first place. I'm reminded of the wise quote from hockey great, Wayne Gretsky, who said, "You miss all of the shots that you never take." Likewise, you miss all of the Amazon customer reviews that you never request.

Depending on how quickly you need to accrue more reviews, make your request once or twice per month. You can ask your fans to take action by sending out a reminder in your email newsletter or posting a request on your social media feeds.

You are asking people to do you a big favor, so use language that is appreciative when making a request for book reviews. For example, use these phrases to initiate your request:

- Make an author happy today!
- I'd like to ask you for a favor.
- If you like my books, here's the best way to thank me.

I like to practice what I preach, so I occasionally ask my email subscribers to post Amazon reviews for my books by placing a brief request in my newsletters. Usually, I'll get a handful of new reviews within the next few days. The best part is that it's free to ask and free to receive. Remember, your fans love you. They want to help, but they need to be reminded of ways they can contribute to your success.

Below is a template you can use to ask your email subscribers or social media followers to write a customer review on Amazon:

Social post headline or email subject line:

"Make an author happy today!"

Message body:

As you probably know, I recently released a new book called, [Insert Title Here.] Did you know that Amazon customer reviews are a powerful motivator to get other people to buy my books? If you've purchased and read my book, it would thrill me if you clicked on the link below and left a review on Amazon's website. It only takes a few minutes to post a couple of sentences that sum up your thoughts. Your help would be greatly appreciated!"

[Insert the link to your book detail page on Amazon]

When you make this polite request to your fans, include an image of your book cover and the exact link to your book detail page. Don't make people search to find your book on Amazon's website. Make it easy for people to leave a review, and they'll make it easier for you to get more reviews.

2. Create a book launch team

A second way to get more Amazon reviews for free is to formalize the process by creating a "book launch team." A book launch team is a group of people you recruit to help conduct marketing activities during the opening period that a new book goes on sale. Most authors recruit launch team members from their email list and social media followers. Rather than randomly ask fans to write reviews as mentioned in the previous section, a book launch team is designed to formalize the process by getting a lot of people to take action all at one time.

The best time to build your launch team is 4 – 6 weeks

before the book release in order to give people time to read your book beforehand. As people join your team, you can send them an advance reader copy of your manuscript as a digital file. Or, if you're traditionally-published, your publisher might send your launch team printed copies of your new book to read in advance.

One of the most important tasks for a book launch team is to post Amazon reviews during the first two weeks after a book is released. If you recruit a large team of people, you can easily hit a goal of 100 customer reviews in a matter of days.

As mentioned earlier, it is not required for the people on your launch team to buy your book in order to leave a review. But, I highly recommend asking your launch team to pre-order or buy your book for two reasons. First, they are your biggest fans, and they should join the campaign to buy your books. Second, the more people who write reviews for your book as a verified Amazon customer, the less concern that Amazon may get concerned and remove any of your book reviews.

I've helped manage major book campaigns with launch teams of 250 – 1,000 people. When everything works according to plan, there can be hundreds of Amazon reviews for shoppers to see within a few days after the book is released. It's like pouring gasoline on a fire. The launch team activity creates the "online crowd" that attracts the attention of other readers and converts them into buyers.

3. Put a review request at the end of your book

This next step is one of the easiest, yet most often ignored, techniques to get a lot of customer reviews for free over the long term. At the end of every book you publish, add a paragraph requesting readers to write a review on Amazon. People rarely write a review unless you make the request obvious for them to see.

When someone finishes reading your book and enjoyed it, capitalize on their satisfaction by putting a request right after you say "The End." If you can get the Amazon link for your book before it goes to print, add it into the manuscript. If you self-publish via Amazon KDP, you can re-upload your book manuscript with a review request at the end that contains the link to your book detail page on Amazon.

Your language doesn't have to be fancy. Simply say:

Make an author happy today! If you enjoyed this book, please consider posting a review. Even if it's only a few sentences, it would be a huge help.

Then, display the link to your specific book page on Amazon.

Almost every book on Amazon has multiple formats, such as paperback, hardcover, and e-book. Customers may click on the different versions of your book to leave a review. But, all reviews are aggregated across all formats of your book by Amazon into one total number for shoppers to see.

4. Tell happy readers to thank you with a review

The fourth way to get more Amazon reviews for free is to harness the enthusiasm of a happy fan who contacts you by surprise. These moments are prime opportunities for success. When someone tells you that they love your book, strike while the iron is hot.

For example, you might receive an email out of the blue from an ecstatic reader. You might receive a message via social media from someone who loves your book. You might even get stopped by someone in public who says, "Are you the author of ___? I really enjoyed your book!"

These situations happen more often than you might think. As an author myself, I've been recognized at multiple gas stations by fans of my books. I was even recognized standing in line at Home Depot store when someone shouted out, "Hey! Are you the guy who wrote that book?" As crazy as it sounds, these moments do occur in the life of an author.

However, when they happen, don't miss the opportunity to use the situation to your advantage. When someone goes out of their way to say thanks, they have self-identified as a fan who is willing to take action. If anyone is likely to give your book a positive review, it is that individual. After you politely say thank you and before you walk away, tell that person the following:

I'm really flattered that you took time to thank me for my book. You just made my day. If I may be honest, one of the best ways you can thank me is to go on Amazon and write a review. If you would feel comfortable doing that today, I'd be grateful.

You can use this same language if someone emails you to

express appreciation for your book. Simply reply to the email and add this message:

I'm so glad you liked my book. One of the best ways you can thank me is to write a review on Amazon. Here's the link for my book on their website...

How Long Will It Take to Get More Reviews?

Once an author becomes convinced of the need for more Amazon reviews, the next question usually becomes how long will it take to reach 100 reviews or more. The answer depends on these factors:

- The size of your current email list or social media following
- The self-esteem to regularly ask readers to post a review
- Your willingness to take the initiative and make reviews a priority

If you already have a large email list or a social media fan base with over 10,000 people, you might make one request and add 100 Amazon reviews in a matter of days. If your fan base is small or you've been uncomfortable asking readers for support, then it may take several months.

The good news is that asking people to write more customer reviews is within your control. When people express an interest in your book, ask them to do you a favor. A small percentage will usually be willing to help. As you continue to ask on a regular basis, that small percentage will add up over time to generate dozens of reviews. Several dozen will eventually lead to 100 or more.

By the way, if your book already has 100 reviews, don't become complacent. The more reviews, the better. Give yourself a new goal, such as 250 or 500 reviews. Nothing attracts a crowd like a really big crowd.

Above all, though, never pay for reviews or use unethical practices. You can get plenty of reviews over time if you use my four free techniques described in this chapter. Ask you fans to help, create a launch team, add a request to the back of your manuscript, and capitalize when unexpected opportunities occur.

By the way, if you find the information in this book helpful, I'd be grateful if you post a review on Amazon. You'd make this author really happy!

3

MAXIMIZE YOUR AUTHOR CENTRAL ACCOUNT

Amazon has a reputation of constantly increasing their market share of book sales and putting financial pressure on publishers and competing retailers. So, it is unlikely that they would be considered a friendly organization by their industry peers. Yet, in many respects, Amazon could be considered a friendly organization towards authors. No one else has developed such a robust online system to aid authors in marketing their books.

The Amazon Author Central account is a prime example of how Amazon can help make an author's life a little easier. But, like many authors whom I've coached, you might not be aware of this helpful resource. Or, you might not know about all the free tools that Amazon makes available. For instance, did you know that the Author Central account includes these features?

- Help Amazon shoppers discover all of the books you've written
- Display author bio, videos, blog posts, and upcoming events
- Check your Nielsen BookScan retail sales history for free
- Add more best seller categories for your books

This chapter removes the mystery of the Author Central account and explains:

- The benefits of creating an Author Central account
- How to complete your account information
- How to use the free data that Amazon provides

To get the most out of this chapter, I recommend using the website link below first and set up your free Author Central account. Once your account is created, use this chapter to go through the details. Go to:

https://authorcentral.amazon.com/

Note: To create your Author Central account, you'll need to enter the username and password from the Amazon account you use to buy products on their website. Have that information ready when you visit the link above. If you don't have an Amazon shopping account, you are a surprisingly rare holdout! Sorry, you'll have to join the ranks of everyone else and set up an Amazon shopping account. But, it's worth doing just to access the free Author Central features.

The Benefits of an Author Central Account

Your Author Central account serves as a "one-stop-shop" for everything about you and your books on Amazon's website. It's like an online store dedicated to everything you've ever written.

Take a moment to consider the size of Amazon's website. It's massive! There are millions of titles already listed for sale, and over a thousand new books are added every day. Based on the colossal scope of Amazon's website, it's easy for you and your books to get lost in the shuffle – even if you're a bestselling author.

Amazon recognized this problem and developed a simple way for authors to carve out space on their website called the "Amazon Author Page." The Author Page is defined as:

"A handy place for customers to learn about you. Helping customers get to know you is an effective way to introduce them to—or better educate them about—all of your books. On the Author Page, we display essential information about authors—including bibliographies, biographies, author photos, and even feeds to blog posts."

To view examples of Amazon Author Pages, click on the links below:

Rob Eagar: https://amazon.com/author/robeagar

Stephen King: https://amazon.com/author/stephenking

By completing the details of your Author Central account, you bring all of your pertinent information into one place.

Then, Amazon is able to present that information to readers in three key ways.

First, a link to your Author Page will appear near the top of search results listings on Amazon's website when shoppers search using your author name. For example, type "Rob Eagar" into Amazon's search field, and you'll see a link for my Author Page displayed near the top.

Second, a link to your Author Page also appears at the top of every book detail page for each of your books on Amazon. You'll usually see a link with your name underneath where your main title is displayed.

Third, Amazon also provides a link to your Author Page that can be embedded on your social media pages, author website pages, or inserted into your email signature file.

Does a one-stop-shop for your books on Amazon really matter? Absolutely. Your Author Page is the best way to cross-promote all of your books to Amazon shoppers.

For example, you probably know that Stephen King is the master of horror who has written dozens of bestselling novels. But, did you know that he also has a very popular non-fiction book that isn't scary at all? One of King's top-selling books on Amazon is a teaching guide for authors called *On Writing*.

I discovered this book by visiting his Author Page on Amazon (see the link to his page listed above). If Stephen King didn't have an Author Page, many Amazon shoppers would never know about his helpful non-fiction book. Stephen King's Author Page displays all of his novels and makes people aware of his non-fiction work as well. Commit this book marketing principle to memory:

People cannot buy what they do not know exists.

If people don't know that one of your books exists, they can not buy it. Therefore, helping people discover all of your books is half the battle to increasing your sales. If you plan to sell more than one book on Amazon, which most authors do, then you need a place where all of your books can be found by readers.

Your Author Central account is an effective way to bring all of your books in one place for readers to see. Amazon is essentially begging you to help them market all of the titles you've written. If the world's largest book retailer makes that kind of request, why on earth would you pass up the opportunity?

If you're a first-time author with only one book, don't feel left out. I assume you have plans for more books in the future. Now is the time to create your Author Central account to help maximize sales for your current book. Plus, it's wise to build a home base on Amazon today in preparation for writing new books down the road.

How to Set Up Your Author Central Account

Once you've created an Author Central account using your Amazon username and password, use this link to access and complete all of your information:

https://authorcentral.amazon.com/

When you log in to your account, you will see the main page that says, "Welcome to Author Central." To be honest, most of the information on this main page is irrelevant, such as the "Author Central News." Instead, focus on the options across the top of the screen that say, "Author Page," "Books," "Sales Info," and "Customer Reviews."

The first step is to click on the "Books" link. In order to set up your Author Page, you must tell Amazon all of the books that belong to you. By clicking on "Books," you enter the part of your author account that builds your bibliography. This brings you to a new page that says "Books by *Your Name.*"

At the top of the "Books" page, you will see a question that says, "Are we missing a book?" If you don't have any books identified yet, or if one of your books is missing from the list on this page, then click on the yellow button that says, "Add more books." This button makes a new window appear that says "Add books to your bibliography."

In this bibliography search window, you can locate any of your books on Amazon's website by title, author name, or ISBN number. Enter the information to find your books, and then click on the button for each book that says, "This is my book." Your book will be automatically added to your Author Central account bibliography within 24 – 48 hours.

Here's the next easy step. After you've added all of your books to your bibliography, go back to the top option of your account that says, "Author Page." This is where you add all of your personal information for shopper to see, such as your author biography, photos, and videos. You can even include a feed from your blog if you have one. To add new information, click on any of the links within each section, such as "edit biography," "add photo," or "add video." It usually takes 24 hours for any new information or updates to appear within your account.

I recommend adding an author photo or video only if you have a high-resolution imagery to display. First impressions matter, so hire a local photographer to take good headshots for you to place on Amazon. And, only upload movies or book trailers that are professional quality.

In addition, you can add upcoming events to your account, such as speaking engagements, book signings, and media interviews. I'll be candid and tell you that very few authors use this feature, probably because few authors conduct live book tours anymore. But, if you have a frequent appearance schedule, your Author Page can help keep some Amazon shoppers aware of your events.

After you add all of your personal information to your Author Page, make sure to review how everything will look to shoppers on Amazon's website. You can preview the way your Author Page will appear by clicking on the link in the top left corner that says, "Visit Amazon's *Your Name* Page." That link will make a new webpage appear that displays your official Amazon Author Page. You are now ready for the public to see your one-stop-shop on Amazon's website. If you see any mistakes or want to add new information in the future, just follow the steps listed above again.

Access Your Nielsen BookScan Sales History

If you're a traditionally-published author or self-published without using Amazon's KDP service, getting timely sales data for your books can be frustrating. Many authors feel like they're working in the dark. How many books did you sell last week? How many books have you sold so far this year? Wouldn't it be great to know that information with the click of a button?

Publishers track the retail sales of all their titles, including books sold through Amazon. But, that information is very expensive to obtain, and they rarely share it with authors. Therefore, many authors have to beg their publisher for updates or wait to receive book sales data in their monthly or quarterly royalty statements. Waiting is such a pain.

Amazon realized this headache and decided to provide authors with the same retail sales data that publishers pay big money to access – for free. Here's how to see it.

When you are logged-in to your Author Central account, click on the link at the top of the screen that says "Sales Info." In the drop-down menu that appears, click on the option that says "NPD BookScan." The next screen that appears will say "BookScan Weekly Sales." On this screen, you will see a chart that shows your print book sales over different time periods from the past.

Amazon shares the NPD BookScan sales information for all paperback and hard cover books (e-books are not included) connected to your Author Central Account. NPD BookScan used to be called Nielsen BookScan, which is considered the industry-leading resource for tracking sales of print books at all major retailers.

Nielsen is the company known for tracking nationwide consumer buying habits, such as household television viewing statistics and trends in the way people purchase packaged goods. When it comes to books, Nielsen's division called NPD BookScan reports nearly 85% of all print book sales in the U.S. According to Amazon's website, the sales figures from BookScan tally up the print sales from more than 10,000 retailers, including:

- Amazon print book sales
- Barnes & Noble
- Deseret Book Company
- Hastings
- Target
- Walmart
- Costco
- Rakuten

However, the BookScan sales figures do NOT include:

- Amazon e-book sales
- Sales to libraries
- Purchases by wholesalers such as Ingram
- Sales of used books
- Fulfillment by Amazon (FBA) sales
- Pre-orders—orders for a book before the book is released

For more details on the BookScan data, visit this link on Amazon's website:

https://authorcentral.amazon.com/gp/help?topicID= 200580390#salesBarChart

Keep in mind that when you look at your BookScan sales in your Author Central account, it only refers to print book sales. E-book sales are not included. I agree that it would be better if Amazon provided both print and e-book sales together. But, that is their decision for now. Regardless, the information on print sales can be beneficial, especially to traditionally-published authors.

In addition, there other benefits of reviewing the BookScan sales data within your Author Central account:

- Review your print book sales data for the past 4 weeks, 8 weeks, 24 weeks, 52 weeks, and 2 years.
- Drill-down to see exactly how many books were sold during each one-week period.
- Use the sales charts to view sales trends over time and identify the highs and lows.
- Identify sales spikes and match those spikes to previous marketing activities, such as an advertising campaign, price discounts, media interviews, etc.
- Compare sales of up to three of your books against each other in your account.
- Use the most recent sales data to estimate a rough ballpark of future royalty payments coming from your publisher.

Besides these useful features, the BookScan data also displays your book sales by geography across America. BookScan divides the country into Designated Market Areas (DMAs). These are the same geographic areas used by The Nielsen Company to track local television viewing. DMAs are organized by zip codes, and are typically named after the largest city within the area. If you're an author who speaks frequently in public or wants to put together a speaking tour, the geographical sales information can help identify cities where more of your readers might congregate.

When you review the BookScan data for your books, the data might feel encouraging or depressing. Regardless, it's always better to work with more information than guessing in the dark. It's a nice gesture by Amazon to provide this expensive sales data to authors for free. Whenever you want to know how many print books you've sold, just log-in to your Author Central account for updates.

How to Review Your Customer Reviews

There is another helpful part of your Author Central account that deserves discussion. The last link at the top of your account home screen will say, "Customer Reviews." If you click on this link, you will see a listing of all the reviews that customers have written for all of your books. You can sort the reviews by individual book, by date, or by rating level.

It may feel a bit daunting to see every public comment ever written about your books on Amazon. For instance, you might be worried about seeing negative reviews or rude comments from people who didn't like your book. The author ego can be a fragile creature.

Here's my contrarian advice: Do not be afraid of negative reviews. In fact, I believe it's advantageous for every book to have some negative reviews. No book is perfect for every person. Having some negative reviews helps legitimize the discussion around your book. If every review is positive, some shoppers will think you just stacked the deck with your family and friends.

Rather than fear negative reviews, your bigger goal is to amass as many total reviews as possible, both good and bad. Shoppers are swayed more by seeing a book with a lot of reviews. Most shoppers realize that not every reader will like your book.

However, there is a difference between a negative review and an abusive review. In today's online culture, some people can feel emboldened by the anonymity that the Internet affords. So, they will make outlandish, rude, and even slanderous comments in a customer review.

Thanks to your Author Central account, you have the ability to tell Amazon if you feel a specific review is unfair or abusive. If Amazon agrees with your complaint, they will remove the review. Follow these steps to report an abusive review to Amazon:

Step 1 – If you see an abusive or inappropriate review listed on the "Customer Reviews" page of your account, click on the link underneath it that says, "View on Amazon." A new webpage will appear that shows that individual review on Amazon's website.

Step 2 – Underneath the review comments, there is a hyperlink with light gray words that says, "Report abuse." Click on that link.

Step 3 – A pop-up window will appear that says, "Report abuse. If you find this content inappropriate and think it should be removed from the Amazon.com site, let us know by clicking the button below." Click on the gold button that says, "Report." Amazon will ask you to enter the reason you believe it violates their guidelines.

Step 4 – If you do not see a "Report abuse" link on the screen, you can also send an email to: community-help@amazon.com. In your message, specify the webpage location of the abusive review and the reason you believe it violates their guidelines.

Amazon will be notified about your concerns over the abusive review and make a decision to delete it or allow it to remain. It's ultimately their decision. But, you never have to accept abusive reviews. Use your Author Central account to contact Amazon if there is a legitimate concern.

Add More Amazon Categories for Your Book

In Chapter 1, I explained the importance of selecting the right categories for your book on Amazon's website. Categories help people find your book when searching for new titles to buy within a specific genre. Plus, books that appear on a Top 100 bestseller list for a category or win the #1 bestseller badge get extra marketing exposure that helps close more book sales.

Therefore, if the Amazon categories you select for your book are incorrect or too few, then many readers may not discover your book while searching on Amazon's website.

Publishers can select up to five categories for a book. Self-published authors who use Amazon's KDP service can select two categories at the time of publication and then add up to 10 total categories after the launch date.

If you'd like to change or add more categories for your book, you can use your Author Central account to contact Amazon and follow these steps to make a request:

Step 1 – Log in to your Author Central Account, and click on "Help" in the top right corner.

Step 2 – On the next screen, click the "Contact Us" button on the left column.

Step 3 – On the "Contact Us" page, click on the menu where it says, "Please make a selection," and then select, "My Books."

Step 4 – A second menu will appear that says, "Select details." Click on the option that says, "Update information about a book."

Step 5 – A third menu will appear that says, "Please make a selection." Select the option that says, "Browse Categories."

Step 6 – Finally, a fourth menu will appear that says, "Please make a selection." Click on the option that says, "I want to update my book's browse categories."

Step 7 – Underneath the fourth menu, a new box will appear that says, "If you'd like to make a change to these categories, please give us a call."

Step 8 – Once you've completed these steps, you will see a new box appear at the bottom of the page that says, "How would you like to contact us?" The options provided include email and phone. If you select the phone option during Amazon's business hours, you can insert your phone number and receive a call back within a few minutes. How cool is that for service?

You can also use the email option to contact Amazon and request a new category for your book. But, I suggest using the phone option to make sure your request is handled correctly and ask any pertinent questions.

Before you contact Amazon, be prepared to provide the Amazon Standard Identification Number (ASIN#) for your book. Their customer service team will need that key piece of information to process your request. You can find the ASIN number on your book's detail page on Amazon under the "Product details" section.

In addition, you will need to provide the specific category details you want to add. For instance, you will need to list the complete category string you want added, starting with "Books" or "Kindle eBooks," such as:

Kindle eBooks > Mystery, Thriller & Suspense > Vigilante Justice

Books > Reference > Writing, Research & Publishing Guides > Writing Skills

When you talk to Amazon, they usually allow you to add up to three new categories per request. So, you might need to repeat the steps above a couple of times to get the maximum number of categories listed for your book. It's worth the extra time to get the additional categories listed in their system. More categories equals more visibility to Amazon shoppers. More visibility helps generate more sales.

As you can see, the "Help" feature within Amazon's Author Central account is a powerful service for authors. Besides requesting changes to your book categories, you can also contact Amazon for assistance in other areas, such as:

- Link customer reviews between different editions of the same book
- Set up an Author Central account in the UK, Germany, and Japan
- Change the book edition that shows up in search results that shoppers see
- Turn on the "Search Inside the Book" feature
- Add a book with a co-author to your account
- Add a book under a pen name to your account

I've found Amazon's customer service team to be quite responsive. Once you create your Author Central account, don't be shy to contact them for help.

Amazon's Author Central account offers too many benefits to ignore. Yet, too many authors never create an account or keep their information updated. Do not overlook the power that Amazon puts into your hands. The Author Central account enables you to:

- Create a "one-stop-shop" for all of your books
- Cross-promote and raise awareness of all your titles
- Track your Nielsen BookScan sales data for free
- Monitor customer reviews and report any abuse
- Add more browse categories for your book

Take time to complete your Author Central account and maximize the way your books are displayed and discovered on Amazon's website.

There is one more major benefit related to your Author Central account that I haven't mentioned yet. Your account gives you the secret ability to update the marketing text for any of your books whenever you desire. But, this feature is such an important topic that I've devoted the entire chapter to the subject. Check out the next chapter, "Amazon's Secret Marketing Back Door," for all of the juicy details.

4

AMAZON'S SECRET MARKETING BACK DOOR

In Chapter 1, I explained the importance of presenting persuasive marketing text on your Amazon book detail page. If you have an effective book detail page, it will help increase your sales. But, if you have a boring book detail page, it can hinder your sales. In addition, we examined stellar samples of fiction and non-fiction book detail pages that you can follow as examples.

After realizing the significance of your book detail page, you may want to make some upgrades and improve your ability to close more book sales. But, there's a problem. You may not know how to access your book detail page and improve the text that shoppers see.

In fact, most authors aren't aware that they can change their book detail pages, because their publisher or a third-party self-publishing company originally listed their book on Amazon.

For instance, you might be a traditionally-published author who desperately wishes you could improve the marketing copy on your Amazon pages. Maybe your publisher created boring text for your book, and you feel helpless to fix the problem. Or, maybe you've won an award or hit a sales milestone, so you'd like to update your book on Amazon with this new information. Maybe you've asked your publisher to make the update, but didn't receive a timely response.

On the other hand, you might be an indie author who self-published using a different company other than Amazon's Kindle Direct Publishing service. You'd like to make some improvements to your book detail page as well. But, are you locked out from accessing your own book on Amazon's website?

- What if you could override your publisher and improve the marketing text yourself?
- What if you could ensure Amazon shoppers see the best promotional copy possible?
- What if you could improve your book's marketing copy whenever you desire for free?

Good news. You can change your book's promotional text on Amazon at any time. Their website has a hidden "back door" that lets any author upload a new book description. This access is available to every author, regardless if you are traditionally-published or self-published.

In this chapter, I'll walk you through the steps to use Amazon's secret marketing back door. My goal is to help you take control over the way your book appears to millions of readers. If more people can see your book with compelling marketing copy, you will sell more books.

Three Reasons to Keep Your Books Updated on Amazon

I'm a firm believer that the author should have control over the way their book appears on Amazon. After all, it's your book. You put more time and effort into the material than anyone else. Also, it might be a primary source of income for you and your family. Thus, there are three reasons why you should always monitor and improve the way your book appears on Amazon's website:

1. Your book's marketing text has a direct influence on your book sales.

Allow me to reiterate that when people view your book on Amazon, your marketing copy will help persuade or dissuade them from making a purchase. If you've got excellent marketing copy, it will encourage people to buy your book. If your marketing copy is boring, the lackluster text can work against you and hinder sales.

2. Different versions of your book need the same marketing text.

In most cases, your book has more than one version on Amazon's website. For instance, your book might have been originally published in hardcover. Then, the paperback version was introduced. Almost every book has an e-book version. Also, many books are now converted into audio format. That's four different versions of the same book on Amazon. But, different people will view the four different versions based on their reading preferences. This leads to a potential problem.

Each version of your book has a completely different webpage on Amazon's site. And, the marketing text doesn't automatically stay the same. You have to make sure it's the same. Plus, publishers are notorious for uploading different types of marketing copy for the same book on Amazon. Yet, most authors fail to double check and make sure their book's marketing text is consistent across all formats.

Look for yourself. Go on Amazon right now, and I'll wager that you will see discrepancies for your book across the different versions. The marketing copy may be different. The text formatting may be dissimilar. You need to examine every version of your book to ensure that shoppers see the most updated and most compelling marketing text.

Does it really matter? Of course. You never know which version will be a reader's first impression of your book. First impressions matter. Therefore, you want the paperback, hardcover, audio, and e-book versions for your books to all have the same persuasive promotional copy.

3. Poor formatting can cost you book sales.

Let's try a little experiment. At the time of this writing, the text listed below is the actual marketing copy pulled from Amazon's website for a book entitled, *Boundaries in Marriage*. When you see all of the words smashed into one giant paragraph, do you feel enticed to read it?

.   .   .

Learn when to say yes and when to say no--to your spouse and to others--to make the most of your marriage. Only when a husband and wife know and respect each other's needs, choices, and freedom can they give themselves freely and lovingly to one another. Boundaries are the "property lines" that define and protect husbands and wives as individuals. Once they are in place, a good marriage can become better, and a less-than-satisfying one can even be saved. Drs. Henry Cloud and John Townsend, counselors and authors of the award-winning bestseller Boundaries, show couples how to apply the 10 laws of boundaries that can make a real difference in relationships. They help husbands and wives understand the friction points or serious hurts and betrayals in their marriage—and move beyond them to the mutual care, respect, affirmation, and intimacy they both long for. Boundaries in Marriage helps couples: • Set and maintain personal boundaries and respect those of their spouse• Establish values that form a godly structure and architecture for their marriage• Protect their marriage from different kinds of "intruders"• Work with a spouse who understands and values boundaries—or work with one who doesn't.

Like me, you probably saw this huge paragraph and felt no desire to read it. All of those words appear as one big blob with no appeal whatsoever. You probably just skipped reading it altogether and jumped to this paragraph.

Imagine how Amazon shoppers feel when they see such a huge chunk of words. Based on this unappealing blob, most people won't take time to read the description for *Boundaries in Marriage*. The few who might try to decipher that paragraph might be someone who received a recommendation for the book via word of mouth or someone who is desperate to fix their marriage. Yet, most shoppers aren't in that position. Most visitors to Amazon's website are browsing without a word of mouth recommendation, nor do they feel any relationship desperation in the moment.

Let's take this example a step further. If you view the e-book version of *Boundaries in Marriage* on Amazon, you will see completely different marketing text. But, it's another large, single paragraph that is frustrating to read. This book has two separate versions with poorly formatted marketing text. Imagine how many sales could have been lost over the years due to this preventable problem.

Am I just splitting hairs and being picky? No, displaying text that is hard to read will prevent some Amazon shoppers from deciding to buy a book. Not everyone will walk away, but why risk losing any sales when the problem is within your control to fix. It's like choosing to shoot yourself in the foot with your own gun. It doesn't make sense.

If you want to sell books to the masses, you must display persuasive marketing copy that the masses can easily read and appreciate. Bad formatting causes people to ignore your book and label it as unprofessional. Any of the issues listed below can hinder your book sales if they appear on Amazon's website:

- Marketing text that is boring and lacks persuasion
- Marketing copy smashed into one big paragraph
- Lack of statements in bold or bulleted lists
- No book hook at the beginning of marketing text

- Lack of displaying persuasive testimonials, endorsements, and awards
- Inconsistent marketing text across various formats of the same book
- Displaying too much marketing text that is overkill rather than concise

Fortunately, Amazon gives every author a way to fix these problems – for free. By now, you may be waiting with baited breath to know the secret. How do you access Amazon's back door? The answer lies inside your Amazon Author Central account.

How to Access Amazon's Secret Back Door

The Amazon Author Central account provides any author access to change their book's marketing copy whenever desired. If you're not familiar with setting up your Author Central Account, I explained all of the details in Chapter 3. Refer to that chapter for instructions to create your account if you haven't already.

After you have your Author Central account set up and your bibliography completed, then follow these 10 steps to access your books and make the desired changes to the marketing text:

Step 1 – Log in to your free account at:

https://authorcentral.amazon.com/

Step 2 – Once inside your account, click on the word at the top that says, "Books."

Step 3 – When you click on "Books," it brings up a new screen with all of the books you've added to your author library. (If you're unfamiliar with adding books to your library, refer back to Chapter 3.)

Step 4 – Choose the book that you want to update the marketing copy. You can click on the title or book cover image displayed to make your selection.

Step 5 – After you select a book, a new webpage will appear that shows all of the details about your book. Scroll down the page and click on the tab that says, "Editorial Reviews."

Step 6 – Under the "Editorial Reviews" tab, scroll down until you see a section labeled, "Product Description." In that section, the marketing copy for your book is displayed.

Step 7 – In most cases, there will be a small button that says "Edit" next to your book's product description. Click on the "Edit" button.

Note: If you do not see an "Edit" button next to your book's product description, there will usually be a link that says, "Request a correction." Click on that link to contact Amazon's customer service team for help. You can send them the updated marketing copy to install for you. Or, you can ask them to reinstall the "Edit" button for your book.

Step 8 – After clicking on the "Edit" button, a new window will pop up on your computer screen that lets you type or paste new marketing copy for your book.

Amazon recommends using a plain text editor, such as Notepad, to paste in new text. Rich text editors, such as Microsoft Word, can cause formatting issues that delay or prevent your update from being processed by Amazon's system.

Step 9 – Type or paste the new marketing copy for your book into Amazon's editing window. Then, select using bolded font, italics, or bulleted lists as needed. When you're finished, click on the "Preview" button at the bottom right corner to see how the changes look before sending them to Amazon.

Step 10 – Once everything looks good to you in the preview window, click on the "Save changes" button to submit the changes to Amazon. Those changes will usually appear on your book's Amazon page within 24 – 48 hours. Now you're in control of your book's success!

To review Amazon's specific guidelines for updating the marketing text for your book, use this link:

https://authorcentral.amazon.com/gp/help?ie=UTF8& topicID=200649600

Remember to update the marketing text for every version of the same book. You can find the different versions listed for each book by going to your book's specific page as mentioned in Step 5 earlier. In the top right corner of every book page, there is a box that says, "Editions," which displays all of a book's editions for sale on Amazon's website. Editions can include hard cover, paperback, e-book, and audio formats. Each edition listed is a hyperlink you can click to access that version's details and make any desired updates.

Besides changing your book's marketing text, you can also use the section listed under the "Editorial Reviews" screen to add new endorsements, industry reviews, or insert your author bio. This is a great way to keep your book updated with the most relevant details and testimonials from influential people.

Now that you know how to access Amazon's secret back door, use it wisely. As you update your books' promotional copy, always lead with your strongest marketing text. For instance, if your book has hit a major bestseller list, show that information first. If you received an endorsement from a famous person or well-known media organization, show that testimonial at the top of your marketing text as well. If you don't have those accolades, put the marketing hook for your book at the top of your description text. Use a bolded font to make all of the words stand out on the page.

If you're a traditionally-published author, you no longer have to beg or wait for your publisher to fix your book's marketing copy. You have the power to update your books at any time and for every version that resides on Amazon's website.

If you're a self-published author who wants to remain competitive in the marketplace, now you have a level playing field. You can make improvements at any time on Amazon. It's a big step forward for author empowerment.

Better marketing copy equals better book sales. The power to display persuasive promotional text for your books is now fully in your hands.

5

UNDERSTANDING THE AMAZON BEST SELLERS RANK

There are few things in an author's life that can generate extreme angst like the Amazon "Best Sellers Rankings." I confess there were times early in my author career when I used to check my book's ranking 10 - 15 times a day. For a while, my wife thought I was obsessed.

I'm not alone. I've met authors who admitted to waking up in the middle of the night and peeking at their book rankings. Due to the emotional stress and confusion that authors may feel, including you, this chapter is meant to clarify what the Amazon Best Sellers Rank means and doesn't mean. Here's what you'll learn in this chapter:

- How to identify the Best Sellers Rank for your book
- How to estimate book sales based on a sales rank
- How to debunk the myth of the Amazon best seller
- How to use sales rankings to aid marketing efforts

What is the Amazon Best Sellers Rank?

In case you're unfamiliar with the Best Sellers Ranking on Amazon's website, here's a basic description. Every hour, Amazon runs a mathematical calculation for every book in their inventory based on recent sales through their website. This calculation compares the sales of one book against all the other books in their inventory to determine which titles are selling the most copies. Every hour, their system does it again.

Amazon keeps the details of their calculation system a closely guarded secret. No one knows exactly how their algorithms work, except a few employees who manage the system. In addition, Amazon routinely changes the algorithm, so their calculation methods never stay the same. Amazon keeps everyone in the dark. So, it's a bit of guessing game to understand how everything works.

Using a basic description, Amazon runs a calculation on every book they sell every hour of the day and gives each book a numerical score called the "Best Sellers Rank." Only one book can receive a score of #1, which means that book was the top-selling title compared to every book on Amazon over the past hour. The higher a book's Best Sellers Rank, the fewer copies that book sold compared to the #1 book in Amazon's inventory. Put simply, the lower the number, the better the sales. The higher the number, the worse the sales.

The purpose of the ranking system is to let Amazon and

their website visitors see which books are currently selling the most copies. In addition, people can see how books are faring against each other from a real-time standpoint. It's fascinating that Amazon invested so much computing power to monitor and compare every unit from their massive inventory. They were smart to share this information with the public. But, that's where the confusion starts. Authors can put more weight on the rankings than they should and misunderstand what the numbers really mean.

To locate the ranking for your book, visit your book detail page and look about halfway down the page to a section called "Product details." This section also lists other book data, such as the publisher name, ISBN number, product dimensions, and average customer reviews score. The last line in this section displays the phrase, "Amazon Best Sellers Rank," with a number listed to the right side.

As I mentioned, Amazon updates their ranking calculations every hour. Therefore, a book's Best Sellers Rank will change hour by hour to reflect new sales or the lack of recent sales. Changes within a few hours can swing quite a bit. For instance, the ranking that you see for your book during one hour can change a lot just a few hours later. It can change even more by the next day or the next week. Your book's Best Sellers Rank is in a constant state of flux. This constant change causes a yo-yo effect that can drive authors crazy and make them addicted to checking their numbers.

How do you correctly interpret what the Best Seller Rank means for your book? Use this rule of thumb:

*The lower the ranking number for your book, the better your
book is selling on Amazon's website.*

The closer you get to #1, the more units your book is selling
relative to all other books on Amazon. The book with a rank
of #1 represents the best selling title in all of Amazon's
inventory for the past hour. If your book's Best Sellers Rank
is close to #1, then your book is performing really well.

In contrast, books that aren't selling well will have a higher
Best Sellers Rank. Since Amazon has millions of books in
their inventory, the rankings go into the millions. For example, you can see books with a ranking way over #1,000,000,
which is a sign that those titles are selling poorly.

The Best Sellers Rank also lets you compare how one
product is selling versus other similar products. For example, Amazon displays sales rankings for just about everything on their website, including computers, baby food,
garden hoses, and books. Every product on Amazon has a
Best Sellers Rank. But, a book's sales rank only reflects the
book category. So, your book's ranking is only compared
against the sales ranking of other books.

If all this geeky information seems a little hard to follow,
hang with me. It gets even more complex. Every version of
your book has a separate Best Sellers Rank. For instance,
the rank for the hardcover version of your book will have a
different rank from the paperback, e-book, and audio
versions. Amazon creates a separate webpage for every
version of your book, and each page displays a separate Best
Sellers Rank.

When you compare how your book is faring against the competition, be sure to look at all of the different versions and rankings to get aa complete picture. You may have to track four different numbers to see how your book is selling in all formats. You can see why so much confusion occurs around these ranking numbers.

Suffice it to say, your book's Amazon Best Sellers Rank is an unreliable number that constantly fluctuates. Based on this unreliability, authors can misunderstand what the numbers actually mean.

For example, you might see your book's ranking suddenly drop from #100,000 down to #10,000 and think you're on the way to getting rich. Or, you might see your ranking number increase from #50,000 to #150,000 and worry that your book sales are dying. Remember it's a short-term number that changes every hour. You can't rely on the number to discern real sales.

Using an analogy, consider how food reacts when you cook it in a microwave oven. When you cook something in a microwave, it heats up really fast. But, when you remove that food from the microwave, it will also cool down fast.

Your Amazon Best Sellers Rank is like a microwave. It can spike really quickly, but it can also fall very fast. Based on this rapid fluctuation, it's not a reliable number to use for gauging legitimate book sales over time. Even if your book gets to #1 on Amazon's website, it only means your book was #1 for just that one hour.

Your book's Best Sellers Rank is only beneficial for judging short-term sales. You cannot use the numbers to analyze sales over a long period of time. If you want a better picture of sales over time, use the Kindle Direct Publishing (KDP) sales dashboard if you self-published a book using Amazon's service. If you're traditionally-published, review the Nielsen BookScan sales data that I described in Chapter 3 available from your Author Central account.

Your Best Seller Rank can be used to gauge the success of a book launch. In these situations, the ranking doesn't tell how many books you've sold. But, it does let you know if your book is moving up to the top spot in your genre. By monitoring the Best Sellers Rank, you can see if a book launch is performing well or needs to be improved. Plus, Amazon will help market a book that reaches the Top 100 list for books within a specific subcategory.

Again, the ranking data doesn't reflect accurate sales. But, it's one of the few ways to judge real-time performance of book sales when you can't get reliable data anywhere else. In the next section, I'll explain how you can use the Best Seller Rank to make an educated guess if you're starving for sales information.

How to Estimate Book Sales Using Your Best Sellers Rank

Be glad that the publishing industry is filled with book geeks. These people, of which I count myself, get a kick out of hyper-analyzing mountains of data to find useful ways to sell more books. Fortunately, a few geeks decided to figure out if they could correlate actual book sales on Amazon using the Best Sellers Rank. I've even conducted my own informal tests with authors and publisher clients.

Amazon never shares exact sales data unless you self-publish a book using their Kindle Direct Publishing platform. If you don't use KDP, then you are left in the dark on the most important information most authors desire: daily book sales. Since that data isn't readily handy, a ballpark idea is better than nothing. That's why I'm comfortable sharing the following information just to help shed a little light on the subject.

By combining results from other studies along with sales data from my author clients, I put together the following charts that reflect ballpark book sales based on your Amazon Best Sellers Rank.

Please note that none of this information reflects accurate book sales. All it can do is give you a rough idea. Do not use this data to assume actual book sales, quote the sales to someone else, or make important business decisions. This information is only for approximating trends, determining a rough idea of your book sales, or passing the time when you're bored on a rainy afternoon.

Below are two charts. The first chart displays rough estimates for the amount of print units (paperback or hard cover) sold based on a book's Amazon Best Sellers Rank:

PRINT BOOK SALES ESTIMATOR

If your book's Amazon Best Sellers Rank is _____, then you might be selling _____.

#10=1,000 books a day

#100=300

#250=200

#1,000=70

#2,500=50 books a day

#5,000=25

#10,000=10

#100,000=1

#150,000+=Less than 1 book a day

Note: This information does not reflect actual sales and is only useful for determining ballpark figures.

Using the chart above, if your book's print Best Sellers Rank is #10, then you might be selling around 1,000 books a day. Bravo! Any author would love to think they're selling 1,000 books in a day. However, notice how quickly the sales drop off as your Best Sellers Rank falls.

Let's say your rank is #1,000. That means you might have sold around 70 copies of your book in one day. If your rank is #10,000, you might have only sold around 10 copies of your book in a single day. And, once your rank gets to 100,000 or higher, you're probably selling one book a day or even less.

∽

E-BOOK SALES ESTIMATOR

The sales rank estimations are a bit different for e-books. To approximate your ebook sales, I combined sales information from my own client sources and coupled that data with information from two fellow Amazon geeks, David Gaughran and Dave Chesson.

David Gaughran has a great book called *Amazon Decoded*, which provides an in-depth explanation of Amazon's algorithms and the Best Seller Rank. I recommend checking out his work at: https://davidgaughran.wordpress.com/

Dave Chesson, founder of Kindlepreneur, offers a wealth of information about Amazon for indie authors along with a handy online calculator that helps estimates book sales based on your Best Sellers Rank. You can check it out at: https://kindlepreneur.com/amazon-kdp-sales-rank-calculator/

If your book's Kindle Best Sellers Rank is _____, then you might be selling _____.

#1 – 5=Over 4,000 books a day

#10 – 20=3,000 – 4,000

#100=1,000

#1,000=120

#5,000=35

#10,000=20

#50,000=5

#100,000=1

#150,000=Less than 1 a day

Using the e-book sales estimation chart, if your e-book's rank in Amazon's Kindle store is #1, you might be selling over 4,000 e-book copies in a day. If your Kindle rank is #100, you might be selling around 1,000 copies of your e-book in a day. Again, notice how quickly sales decline as your e-book rank drops. If your Kindle rank is #10,000, you've sold an estimated 20 copies in a day. If your ranking goes to #100,000 or worse, you're probably selling one copy or less of your book a day.

As a reminder, these sales estimators are only useful for ballpark guesses and do not represent accurate sale data. The key to making good decisions is to use good information. Fortunately, there are multiple sources you can pursue to get better sales reports.

First, as mentioned in Chapter 3, Amazon provides all authors with the BookScan sales figures for their print books within the Author Central account. The BookScan data covers about 85% of retail print sales but does not include e-books. Yet, it's better than nothing, and you can check it for free at any time using Author Central.

Second, indie authors who use Amazon's Kindle Direct Publishing (KDP) service can get accurate sales reports from their account dashboard. The sales data within that system is usually updated within 24 hours. Plus, KDP lets you create paperback books. So, you can get trustworthy e-book and paperback sales in one place.

Third, if you're a traditionally-published author, you can bug your publisher to send you updated sales numbers.

The bottom line is that real-time sales data is nearly impossible for authors to get. Thus, the Amazon Best Sellers Rank is one of the few tools available for that purpose. But, use it in the right context. Please don't get up in the middle of the night to check your ranking. Otherwise, you might hurt yourself in the dark or get accused of being freakishly obsessed by your spouse.

The Myth of the Amazon Best Seller

As Amazon's dominance took over the publishing industry, an increasing number of authors have tried to use Amazon's influence to boost their credibility. For example, you may have seen an author touting that he or she is a "#1 Amazon Bestseller" on their website or added "Amazon bestseller" to their author bio.

In reality, these authors may have hit the #1 position in an obscure book category on Amazon's website for one hour on a random day. As mentioned earlier, there are thousands of peculiar sub-categories on Amazon, such as "Amish Romance," "Religious Counseling," and "Juices and Smoothies." Getting to the top of these little-known categories is nowhere close to landing on a legitimate bestseller list.

When the average person hears the word "bestseller," they think of the national bestseller lists, such as *The New York Times, USA Today, The Wall Street Journal,* and *Publishers Weekly.* These lists track an entire week's worth of sales by pulling data from several retail outlets, including Amazon, Barnes & Nobles stores, and independent bookstores across America. Typically, a book must sell several thousand copies in one week to qualify for these lists. To hit the #1 slot, a book must usually sell over 10,000 copies.

In contrast, an Amazon category ranking is a quick measure of sales just for one hour on their website. A book may only sell a few dozen units or a few hundred copies to hit #1 in an Amazon category. That's a big difference from the genuine bestseller lists.

Therefore, telling someone your book is an Amazon best-seller is a misleading statement, because there is only one true bestseller list on Amazon's website, which is called "Amazon Charts" (https://www.amazon.com/charts).

Amazon Charts is the company's only official bestseller list, where they track the "Top 20 Most Sold" and "Top 20 Most Read" books over a one-week period. These books are selling thousands of copies consistently over a 7-day period, which is similar to the national bestseller lists. There are separate lists of fiction and non-fiction books. Unless your book appears on the Top 20 Amazon Charts, you shouldn't call yourself an "Amazon bestseller."

Making the ridiculous claim to be an "Amazon bestseller" is irrelevant and misleading to the reading public. Why? Telling people you were #1 in an obscure category on

Amazon's website does not equate to massive book sales. As I just mentioned, it usually means you sold a few hundred copies, which is too few to matter. Plus, I explained in the previous section of this chapter that the Amazon Best Sellers Rank only tracks sales based on a one-hour time period.

Look at it this way. An author who claims to be an "Amazon bestseller" is no different than me claiming to be the fastest runner in my neighborhood for one hour on a Wednesday afternoon. It's an irrelevant claim that makes no sense.

You might be thinking, "Get off your soap box, Rob. Why make such a fuss?" I'm a consultant. It is a consultant's job to ruffle feathers in order to maintain the integrity of our author community. If I ruffled your feathers, so be it. Save any bestseller claims for the legitimate bestseller lists. Otherwise, we all look like fools.

Use Your Sales Rank to Assist Marketing Efforts

Besides providing a ballpark estimate of sales, your book's Amazon Best Sellers Rank can also assist with your marketing efforts.

For instance, your sales ranking can help identify if a specific marketing activity is making an immediate impact on your book campaign. That's because it's one of the few real-time pieces of data available. If you see your sales ranking dramatically improve within a 24-hour period, you can deduce that a recent marketing activity or some word of mouth had a positive impact.

Here's an example of what I mean. Recently, I worked on a major book launch for a client who is a well-known life coach and Hollywood movie producer. As I monitored the Amazon Best Sellers Rank for my client's book, one day I noticed that it quickly dropped from #2,500 down to #141. That dramatic change in the book's ranking signaled that a lot of new sales were occurring.

My client was conducting an active media tour to promote his book over several weeks. But, he was giving so many interviews that we couldn't keep up with his schedule. In addition, not all media is the same. Some interviews get more traction than others. I wanted to identify exactly what type of media interview caused such a great response.

So, when I noticed the big change in my client's Amazon rank, I texted him and asked, "Your book sales just jumped up a notch! What interviews did you do in the past 24 hours?" He replied that a national radio station had interviewed him about his book. And, he was told that radio station added his interview to their YouTube channel that had a large following.

I quickly searched YouTube, found his interview online, and noticed that it had already been viewed over 100,000 times in less than 24 hours! That video interview was the catalyst driving an immediate surge of book sales. Based on that discovery, we followed up to drive more attention to that persuasive video. We posted clips from the interview on his Facebook page. We sent parts of the video to his email list. And, we added the video to my client's author website. Since then, the video has been viewed over 280,000 times and continues to help drive more book sales.

But, I never would have identified this incredible marketing video without seeing the dramatic change in the Amazon Best Sellers Rank for my client's book. The sudden spike alerted me to the clues I needed to discover the video and use it to help my client maximize his book sales.

Likewise, you can benefit by monitoring your book's Best Seller Rank and watching for sudden spikes. If you notice a dramatic improvement, quickly analyze what marketing activities you conducted in the past 24 – 48 hours. That analysis may help explain which marketing activities best motivated readers to buy your book. Those are the activities you want duplicate and repeat on a frequent basis.

For instance, you may see a sudden improvement in your book's Amazon rank after sending out an email blast, conducting an interview, posting a video on social media, speaking in public, or starting a new ad campaign. If you connect the dots to identify what marketing activity caused the Best Seller Rank to suddenly spike, then you've discovered valuable sales information. You know exactly what to do to generate a response from your audience. You may also uncover the exact language that readers find the most persuasive.

Identifying the marketing activities that causes readers to buy books is vital to success. Once you know what works, you can use it repeatedly to help transform a mediocre book launch into a bestselling campaign.

There can be a lot of confusion surrounding the Amazon Best Seller Rank. It's not an accurate indicator of true sales, and it should never be used to claim being an "Amazon bestseller." However, your book's ranking can unlock helpful information to deduce ballpark sales and monitor sudden sales spikes that occur.

Side note: Some authors reading this chapter may have noticed that I only talked about the Amazon Best Sellers Rank. Yet, wherever you see the ranking number displayed on Amazon's website, underneath there are three rows of categories and corresponding numbers. Don't get these items confused.

The Best Sellers Rank is a judge of performance against the entire inventory of every book that Amazon sells. Whereas, Amazon also has thousands of sub-categories for each type of book they sell, such as "Mysteries and Thrillers," "Marriage and Relationships" and even "Children's Facts of Life." For our discussion in this chapter, I avoided talking about the sub-category details in order to prevent confusion.

However, selecting the right categories for your book and monitoring their performance also provides helpful data to gauge your book's performance. For details on Amazon's the sub-categories, refer back to Chapter 1 – "Master Your Book Detail Page."

6

USE AMAZON ADS TO YOUR ADVANTAGE

Amazon sells the largest inventory of books on the planet. We're talking millions of titles available with over 1,000 new books added each day. Shoppers have such a massive selection of titles to browse, how on earth do you make sure that your book gets noticed? Two words:

Amazon advertising

The core purpose of advertising is to get exposure for your books in front of the people most likely to purchase. Since Amazon sells more books than anyone else, their website is logical choice for authors to buy that much-needed exposure.

I consult with top publishing houses that spend thousands of dollars on Amazon ads every day. These publishers survive on razor-thin profit margins. But, they keep buying ads, because they work so well. They make more money on book purchases than they spend on advertising, so they turn a profit.

Today, indie authors who self-publish using Amazon's KDP system can also take advantage of Amazon ads. This is a huge development, because it levels the playing field between upstart indie authors and the old school publishers. For example, superstar indie novelist, Mark Dawson, made over $1.5 million in book royalties in 2019. One of his top strategies for success is buying Amazon ads.

Why are Amazon ads so effective? People who browse Amazon's website are already in a mindset to purchase. All they have to do is see the product they want and click the "Add to Cart" button.

That's not the case with buying ads on Facebook or other social media platforms. People on Facebook are usually checking the latest news, watching cat videos, or lusting over their friend's glorious-looking vacation photos. Most people on social media are distracted and aren't necessarily in the mood to buy something.

In contrast, people on Amazon are active shoppers who can quickly purchase a book at any moment. And, if they're a member of Amazon Prime, they get two-day shipping for free.

The facts are undeniable. Amazon attracts the largest audience of readers. Amazon offers the largest selection of titles. Amazon developed the easiest way to buy books and offers the fastest delivery. Therefore, Amazon is the best place for authors to find new readers and generate more sales. When you combine these facts with an easy-to-use online advertising system, it's a no-brainer. Amazon ads make sense.

In this chapter, I'll explain the following about Amazon ads:

- Six benefits of Amazon ads
- Who can buy Amazon ads
- Two types of Amazon ads available to authors
- How to choose effective keywords
- How to write persuasive ad copy

Note: In my experience, some authors learn better by watching video demonstrations of how to create Amazon ads. If you fall into that camp, I teach an online video course called *Mastering Amazon for Authors* packed with advanced techniques to buy effective ads. Learn more at my website:

http://www.RobEagar.com/courses

Otherwise, this chapter provides a basic explanation of how the advertising system works.

Let's start by looking at the unique benefits that Amazon ads offer to authors.

Six Benefits of Amazon Ads

Amazon offers authors an effective advertising system for fiction and nonfiction books through their division called Amazon Marketing Services (AMS). To setup an account for buying ads, use this link to access the AMS website:

https://advertising.amazon.com/books

Advertising a book on Amazon includes these six unique benefits:

1. Amazon ads only charge on a pay-per-click basis.

Pay-per-click means that if no one clicks on your ad, then you don't get charged. Therefore, you aren't penalized if people don't see your ad, gloss over it, or get distracted. Someone has to actually click on your ad and go to your specific book detail page in order for your credit card to be charged. This benefit prevents your budget from being wasted.

2. Amazon ads give thousands of impressions for free.

Since Amazon only charges on a pay-per-click basis, authors can get thousands of impressions for free. When your ad appears on someone's computer screen, Amazon counts that view as an "impression." Even if people don't click on your ad, they can still see it. Your Amazon ad puts your book title, book cover, and author name in front of people, which helps build author discovery and brand awareness. Sometimes, half of the battle is just getting your book in front of shoppers.

3. Amazon ads are easy to create.

Compared to buying ads on Facebook, Amazon ads are a breeze to set up and monitor. Only five simple steps are required. First, choose what type of ad you want to buy. Second, choose the book you want to promote. Third, select the keywords to target your ad. Fourth, set your budget and bid price. Then, finish by writing a short 30-word marketing hook for your ad. You're done. It's that simple.

4. Amazon ads are inexpensive.

If you're an author on a tight budget, Amazon lets you buy advertising for as little as $1.00 a day. In addition, you can set bid prices for your ad as low as $.15 - $.50 per click. Obviously, the more you spend, the better your results. But, Amazon's entry-level pricing is dirt cheap.

5. Amazon won't waste your budget.

Amazon rarely spends all of the daily budget that you set. For instance, if you set a daily budget of $5.00, Amazon may only spend $3.00 - $4.00 of the total amount. So, you will have a little money left over that can be saved to buy additional ads.

Occasionally, I receive emails from Amazon telling me that an ad has reached the daily budget limit and I should increase my expenditure. That means my ads are being viewed by a lot of readers, so spending more money could yield more results. But, I like that Amazon lets me make that decision myself.

6. Amazon ads are simple to test and adjust.

Successful advertising requires constant testing to determine what works best. On Amazon, it's easy to create several ads simultaneously, change various keywords and bid prices, and then examine which version get the best results. Select the ad you want to test, click the "Copy" button, make the desired changes, then hit "Save." This simplicity is a great feature, especially for authors just getting started with online advertising.

Who Can Buy Amazon Ads?

Amazon ads are currently available to two groups within the publishing industry:

1. Publishing houses who sell books on Amazon

2. Self-published authors who use Amazon Kindle Direct Publishing (KDP)

Note: Authors with an Amazon Advantage account can also buy ads. But, the Advantage account is primarily for self-published authors who want to sell their own paperback inventory through Amazon's website.

There's a logical reason why Amazon ads are limited to the two groups above. They are the only ones who can feasibly turn a profit. You may have noticed that I didn't list traditionally-published authors. Follow this example to understand why.

Most traditionally-published authors receive a royalty payment of $1.00 – $2.00 from their publisher every time a book sells. Amazon ads usually cost $.25 - $.50 per click. That's cheap in the advertising world, but not every click produces a sale. Let's say you sell a book once every 5 clicks, and the average cost per click is $.33. At 5 clicks, that means you paid Amazon $1.65 in ad fees to make a $1.00 royalty from your publisher. When you do the math, your net loss is $.65. That's why it's nearly impossible to turn a profit on Amazon ads when you only get a $1 royalty.

In contrast, publishers and self-published authors make a lot more money each time a book sells. Publishers usually make 45 – 55% of the book's sale price. Authors who self-publish via Amazon's KDP service receive royalty rates of 35% - 70% from the book's sale price.

If a self-published KDP author sells a book on Amazon for $3.99 and gets a 70% royalty, that yields $2.79. With that amount of money, there is room to buy Amazon ads and still turn a profit. Using the same figures from the previous example, one click costs $.33. If a book is sold every 5 clicks, then the advertising expense is $1.65. At that level, the math works in favor of the self-published author ($2.79 royalty – $1.65 ad expense = $1.14 profit). Therefore, publishing houses and KDP authors can afford the expense of Amazon ads and still turn a profit.

However, this doesn't mean traditionally-published authors should avoid using Amazon ads. They can still be a profitable marketing tool. Here are two steps any traditionally-published author can take to get the benefits of Amazon ads:

1. Ask your publisher to buy Amazon ads for your book.

Yes, this option actually works. Several of my author clients have asked their publisher to buy Amazon ads for their books and got a positive response. Most publishers already use the platform. But, you want to make sure they're using it to help sell your books.

Contact your publisher by phone or email and politely ask, "Based on the marketing budget you set for my book, I'd like a portion to go towards Amazon ads. Since Amazon ads would benefit both you and me, would you honor that request?" Amazon ads are inexpensive. Plus, your publisher stands to make a larger profit than you will. So, it's reasonable to ask for them to make the investment on your behalf.

2. Self-publish a book using Amazon KDP and buy ads for that title.

Regardless if your publisher agrees to buy Amazon ads for you or not, consider self-publishing a book via KDP just to get advertising access for yourself. There is no cost to publish books on the KDP platform and the system is easy to use. To set up a free account, use this link:

https://kdp.amazon.com

For example, if you're a traditionally-published novelist, self-publish a prequel or novella using KDP. Within those books, insert links and sample chapters to your traditionally-published books. Then, buy Amazon ads for your KDP titles. Those ads will drive more traffic to your self-published books, which act as a gateway to all of your titles. If you set a daily ad budget of $5.00, that's a smart investment to gain more exposure for all of your books.

If you're a traditionally-published author who writes nonfiction, take a similar approach and self-publish spinoff resources with KDP. For example, you could transcribe a speaking presentation, an audio podcast, or a video course, and turn it into a self-published book. Add links and promotional text within that title that cross-promote all of your other published books. Then, buy ads to attract the specific type of readers who would like everything you've written.

Here's another sly secret: You can create self-published books using KDP as a free way to build your author email list. I will cover all of the details of that technique next in Chapter 7 – "Build Your Email List on Amazon for Free."

Note: In this chapter, I use the term "traditionally-published author" to describe any author who receives an advance or a royalty from a publishing company to publish their book. In the context of Amazon ads, this term would also apply to authors who pay a third-party company to publish their book. These companies are also known as "vanity presses" or "hybrid publishers." In both cases, you would not be able to access Amazon ads unless you self-publish using Amazon's KDP service or set up a specialized Amazon Advantage account.

The Two Types of Amazon Ads

There are two types of ads that Amazon offers to authors:

1. Sponsored Products Ads
2. Lockscreen Ads

To see examples of where Amazon ads appear on their website, click on this link to view visual samples:

https://advertising.amazon.com/kdp-authors

Here's the breakdown of differences between the two types of ads according to Amazon's website:

"Sponsored Products (eBook and paperback) promote individual titles to readers as they search for books. Sponsored Products are targeted by keywords or products. They appear within search results and on product detail pages across desktop and mobile."

"Lockscreen Ads (eBook only) are pay-per-click, interest-targeted display ads that appear on Kindle E-reader and Fire tablet lockscreens and Kindle E-reader home screens. Lockscreen Ads reach customers on their devices, where they are reading and making eBook-purchasing decisions. Ads are targeted by genre interests."

In case you're curious, there are two other types of advertising options on Amazon called "Sponsored Brands Ads" and "Display Ads." A Sponsored Brands Ad appears at the top of search results pages in a separate box with the publisher's name displayed and the option to show 1 – 3 books together. A Display Ad appears on the left-side column of search results pages in a vertical box. However, these two ad options are only available to book publishers or authors with a special Amazon Advantage account.

As a quick aside, whenever you see the words, "Sponsored" or "Sponsored products," on Amazon's website, it is their sneaky way of saying, "You're looking at an advertisement."

For authors, the big difference between Sponsored Product Ads and Lockscreen Ads is where they appear in the buying process. In my opinion, the most important part of the buying process is the beginning, when shoppers are searching for a new book to purchase. To increase the odds that your book is selected, you want your ad to be one of the first items that readers see. That's the advantage of buying a Sponsored Product Ad.

For instance, if a reader types a search phrase into Amazon, such as "military mystery," "marriage advice," or "beach reads," a Sponsored Product Ad promoting a book related to those search phrases will appear. The caveat is that you must include those keywords when you create your ad. But, I'll cover those details later in this chapter.

The Benefits of Sponsored Product Ads

When used correctly, Sponsored Product Ads enable your book to appear first in line for a reader's consideration. When people search for a book in your genre, buying ads increases your ability to appear at the top of the search results list. It's like giving your book a way to cut in line in front of thousands of other competitive titles.

In addition, a Sponsored Product Ad can appear on the book detail pages for other titles that are similar to your book. Typically, these ads appear about halfway down the book detail page underneath the book description text but above the publisher information. You will see a horizontal row of books that says, "Sponsored products related to this item." All of the books appearing in that row are ads that other authors and publishers have purchased.

Why is it beneficial for an ad to appear on another book's

detail page? Let's say an Amazon shopper doesn't see your ad on the initial search results page. Or, maybe they see your ad but choose not to click on it. Wouldn't you love a second chance to get their attention? That second chance occurs when your Sponsored Product Ad appears on the book detail page for another book that the shopper selects.

Amazon lets you target your biggest competitors by using their author names and book titles as keywords you set for your ad. Thus, if someone chooses to visit the book page for your competitor, you can tell Amazon to make a Sponsored Product Ad for your book appear on that competitor's page.

For example, if someone types the search phrase "Lee Child" or "Jack Reacher" on Amazon's website, your Sponsored Product ad might show within the search results that appear. But, if that person clicks on one of Lee Child's books, such as *A Wanted Man*, your Sponsored Product ad can also appear on the book detail page for *A Wanted Man*. Plus, you can place marketing text within your ad that says, "Love Jack Reacher or Lee Child thrillers? Discover the new unstoppable assassin, Harry Mann!" Thus, you can try to woo fans of Lee Child to try your books.

All Amazon ads work on an auction bidding system. Whoever bids the highest price per click wins the opportunity for their ad to appear in front of Amazon shoppers. If you want to make sure your ad appears at the top of search results page or on a competitor's book detail page, you can choose between "fixed bidding" or "dynamic bidding."

"Fixed bidding" enables you to tell Amazon the exact bid that you're willing to be charged if someone clicks on your ad. Your bid price will stay the same throughout the ad campaign. This option enables you to maintain complete control over the bid price that makes you feel comfortable.

"Dynamic bidding" enables Amazon to raise or lower your bid in real time to help your ad be seen by more shoppers. The purpose of this option is to let Amazon use their complex algorithms to identify more opportunities to display your ad and convert a sale. However, the downside is that Amazon can raise your bid price by up to 100%.

For example, if you set a bid amount of $1.00 using the "dynamic bidding" option, Amazon is granted permission to raise your bid up as high as $2.00. By giving Amazon a higher bid range to use, you allow their system to pursue more exposure for your ad and convert more sales.

What if you want to make sure your ad receives the top placement for a specific search result? Amazon also offers an additional bidding option called "Adjust bids by placement," which replaced an earlier feature called Bid+. "Adjust bids by placement" enables you to increase your bid by up to a whopping 900%!

Let's imagine that you want your book to receive the top slot for an Amazon search result when people type in the phrases, "English Regency fiction" or "How to speak Spanish." Those are competitive search terms, which means your ad is vying against hundreds of other ads for the same placement. If you want to ensure your ad wins the top search result position, Amazon will let you raise your bid by up to 900% to secure that slot.

For example, if you set an original bid of $1.00, your ad may not win the most coveted advertising slots on Amazon's website because the bid is too low. Using the "adjust bids by placement" feature, Amazon will let you increase your $1.00 bid by up to 900%, which means your bid could go as high as $10.00 per click! That's a radical example, but it shows how Amazon will let you pay for the top advertising slot if you're willing to part with more money.

IMPORTANT: Always keep in mind that making higher bids can destroy your profit margin and cause your ad campaigns to lose money. Based on my experience, most authors need to keep their bid prices between $.15 - $.75 in order to maintain a healthy profit over time.

If you use Sponsored Product Ads with a wise bidding strategy, it's like getting two chances to advertise for the price of one. Your book ad can appear on a shopper's search result screen or in the middle of another book's detail page. Best of all, you only get charged if someone clicks on your ad. All of the ad impressions on Amazon are free. What a bargain!

The Benefits of Lockscreen Ads

The second advertising option that Amazon offers to KDP self-published authors is called a Lockscreen Ad. But, this type of ad doesn't appear on Amazon's website. Instead, Lockscreen Ads appear on the home page or "lock screen" of Amazon's various Kindle e-reader devices and Fire tablets. To be candid, I don't find Lockscreen Ads to be as productive as Sponsored Product Ads for two reasons:

1. Sponsored Product Ads appear within a shopper's search results. Lockscreen Ads do not.

2. Sponsored Product Ads can also appear the book detail pages of your competition. Lockscreen Ads do not. They only appear on Amazon devices.

However, there is one benefit that is unique to Lockscreen Ads. If you're a novelist, many popular fiction genres, such as mystery, thrillers, sci-fi, and romance, have avid readers who consume a lot of books on their Kindle tablets. By purchasing a Lockscreen Ad, you can reach these high-volume buyers without them having to leave their devices. Your book appears as a featured ad on their screen. With a few simple clicks, users can quickly purchase a copy from Amazon while remaining on the device.

Amazon ads are so affordable that I recommend running tests with both types of ads. Purchase a Sponsored Product Ad and a Lockscreen Ad for your book and measure which type yields the best results. After you test the ads for a few weeks, then you can narrow down and spend your budget on the ad type that works best for you.

How to Target the Right Readers

A successful ad campaign depends upon targeting the right readers. In this regard, Amazon offers two options: automatic targeting and manual targeting.

"Automatic targeting" means Amazon will use their proprietary algorithms to place your book in front of readers who are likely to buy. It's not a perfect system, but it does provide a great way for beginners to get comfortable buying ads.

On the other hand, "manual targeting" enables experienced authors to take full control over the targeting function and make decisions on their own.

If you're new to Amazon ads and just want to get your feet wet, then consider these two options for beginners. I've used these approaches with numerous authors to set up new ad campaigns:

1. Select "Automatic Targeting" and let Amazon do the work for you.

Amazon knows that buying online ads can be complicated. But, they offer a way to simplify the process.

When you create a new "Sponsored Product" ad, select the "automatic targeting" feature and let Amazon do the hard work for you. They already have a mountain of data compiled about people who like to buy books within every genre. They've been tracking that information for years and adding it to their algorithms.

In essence, they know more about people's book-buying habits than anyone else. So, their "automatic targeting" feature is a great time-saver and a smart way to get good results for your ad.

For myself and most of my clients, Amazon ads that use the "automatic targeting" feature produce the most book sales for the least effort.

2. Select "Manual Targeting" and choose keywords based on your biggest competitors.

Besides letting Amazon manage the targeting details for an ad, you can set the parameters yourself. One of the best techniques for success is to set your targeting criteria using keywords based on your top competition. Here's how the strategy works.

A "keyword" is any word, phrase, author name, book title, or genre category that you select to tell Amazon how to show your ad to the appropriate shoppers. You insert the keywords into Amazon's advertising system when creating a Sponsored Product Ad with "manual targeting."

Amazon recommends that you use at least 100 keywords to make the ad as productive as possible. But, how do you come up with 100 effective keywords for your book? Follow these five steps to target your top competitors:

1. Go to your book detail page on Amazon.

2. Scroll down that page to a section that says, "Customers who bought this item also bought…"

3. In that section, Amazon will display several books that customers bought who also purchased your book.

4. Copy the author names and book titles for those other books and paste them into your keyword list for an Amazon ad. The readers of those competitive authors and book titles represent probable candidates who would enjoy your book. Clever, eh?

5. Next, go to your Author Page on Amazon's website. Midway down the left-side column, there will be a section that says, "Customers also bought items by..." In that section, Amazon will display several authors who write similar books in your genre. Copy those author names into your keyword list for an Amazon ad.

Choosing keywords based on competitive author names and book titles helps Amazon display your ad only to readers who prefer your specific genre. This technique increases the likelihood that someone who sees your ad would be interested in your book. If you want your ad to show up in front of the right readers, they tend to be fans of similar authors and titles in your same genre.

What if you're a first-time author and don't have any books listed on Amazon? How do you choose keywords when you have no sales history within Amazon's system? Use the following two techniques:

1. Search for books on Amazon that you think are the most similar to your title. Scroll down to the Best Seller Rank for those books and click on the Top 100 category lists related to those books. Look through the titles displayed on the Top 100 lists and add the top 20 authors' names and book titles to your keyword list. Don't limit your list to just 5 – 10 options. Keep searching until you have at least 50 different names and titles. You can do this research on Amazon's website in less than 30 minutes.

Copy all of the relevant author names and book titles into an Excel spreadsheet or Google document and save it. Then, create a Sponsored Product Ad, select the "Manual

Targeting" option, and paste the information from your spreadsheet into the box that says, "Enter keywords."

2. Identify specific phrases or interests that readers might type into Amazon's search field related to your book. For example, if you write mystery and suspense novels, people might type these phrases into Amazon's search field:

mystery books

mystery best sellers

mystery books with humor

murder mystery

suspense novels

suspense novels under 5 dollars

If you write nonfiction books based on leadership issues, people might type these phrases into Amazon's search field:

leadership books

leadership in crisis

leadership coaching

leadership development

leadership for dummies

leadership best sellers

leadership gifts for employees

Add all of the phrases based on reader interests for your book to your keyword list. The wider your options, the greater chance that your ad will be viewed by more people. More views lead to more clicks on your ad. More clicks on your ad lead to more book sales.

To be clear, don't make your keyword list too narrow. For instance, don't settle for using just 5 or 10 keywords. Amazon recommends using at least 100 keywords to maximize results. Amazon has the power to process all of those options and get your ad in front of the right buyers.

Worried about wasting money on the wrong keywords? Once your ad has run for a few weeks, Amazon will show you which keywords perform best, so that you can remove the poor performers and focus on the keywords that get results. But, you must educate their algorithms accurately with enough keywords during the creation of your ad to optimize success.

Note: If you want to manually select keywords for your ad, use the Sponsored Product Ad option. Lockscreen Ads only let you target by using product categories.

Once you enter the world of Amazon advertising, you can easily get overwhelmed with questions, such as:

- How do you select a winning bid strategy?
- How do you scale your ad budget for better results?
- How do you calculate your return on investment?

Answering these topics is best served by going inside Amazon's advertising system to explain all of the details.

Since that visual information can't be displayed in a book, I offer an online video course called **Mastering Amazon for Authors**, which provides advanced tips and best practices. Get details about this course on my website at:

http://www.RobEagar.com/courses

How to Write Persuasive Amazon Ad Copy

Getting people to see your Amazon ad is only half the battle to winning the book sale. The other half is convincing people to click on the ad and visit your book page. The first battle is won with keywords. The second battle is won with marketing words, also known on Amazon as "custom text." These are the words displayed on your ad to generate curiosity and interest in your book.

However, you only get 150 characters for your "custom text." A limit of 150 characters equates to around 30 words or less. How do you create an attention-grabbing hook in that tiny amount of space?

I recommend the simple technique that I discussed in Chapter 1 using the question, *"What if I told you?"* In essence, start the idea for your custom text with a "what if" question and then fill in the blank. Imagine someone seeing your ad and reading, "What if I told you..." followed by an enticing hook. Below are examples of fiction book hooks using the "what if" approach:

What if a man with amnesia has forgotten he's the world's most dangerous assassin?

What if you must choose between saving your children or hundreds of strangers you barely know?

What if the first astronaut to walk on Mars discovers he might be the first person to die there?

Notice how these hooks catch your attention by using the power of suspense. The same dynamic can work for non-fiction books as well. Below are examples of custom text for Amazon ads using the "what if" technique:

What if I told you everyone speaks, but not everyone is heard?

What if I told you it's possible to cure the disease to please other people?

What if I told you there are 10 simple tactics to triple your productivity?

What if it's possible to teach your special needs child better than any public school?"

The "what if" technique is a great way to spark ideas for custom text that grabs the attention of an Amazon shopper. Also, if you run out of words and need to shorten your text, just remove the "what if" part and and turn your question into a statement, such as:

What if I told you everyone speaks, but not everyone is heard? That question can be shortened to a statement: *Everyone speaks, but not everyone is heard.*

Another effective technique for creating custom ad text is to connect your book to a bestselling author in your genre. For example, your ad copy could say:

Waiting for more John Grisham? Read this page-turning legal thriller with an unforgettable hero.

A nonstop thrill ride for fans of Tom Clancy! To protect his country, Joe Wolf must stop an assassin closing in for the kill or die trying.

Language is the power of the sale. The keywords you select help present your Amazon ads to the right readers. The custom text you insert into your ad helps pique their curiosity to visit your book detail page on Amazon and make a purchase.

If you want to attract readers to your books on a limited budget, there is no better option than Amazon ads. Where else can you get effective promotion for just $5.00 a day? Amazon shoppers are already in a position to buy your book with the quick click of a button.

Even if you're a traditionally-published author, ask your publisher to buy ads on your behalf or self-publish via Amazon's KDP platform to gain direct access to ads yourself.

Use the techniques described in this chapter to maximize the unique benefits of Amazon ads, understand the differences between Sponsored Product Ads and Lockscreen Ads, choose effective keywords, and write persuasive text for your ad. If you want to go deeper and watch video tutorials that explain Amazon's advertising system in complete detail, check out my online course, *Mastering Amazon for Authors*, at:

http://www.RobEagar.com/courses

Amazon ads have leveled the playing field for all authors. Put their power to use and win the game for your book.

7

HOW TO BUILD YOUR EMAIL LIST USING AMAZON

Authors routinely ask me, "What is the single best marketing tactic to sell more books?" I always answer with one word: Email.

Repeated research continues to prove that email marketing is 10 - 20 times better at selling books directly to fans than all social media combined. Therefore, every author needs a bigger email list. If you don't believe me, please read my book, *The Author's Guide to Email Marketing*. You'll be convinced by all of the proof that I present.

But, you might be thinking, "Rob, what does email marketing have to do with Amazon? Are you suggesting they'll share their customer email addresses with me?" No, Amazon doesn't share their customer data with anyone. But, they sell more books than anyone else, and they also attract the largest amount of avid readers. What if you could recruit some of those avid readers to join your email list? Even better, what if you could do it for free?

In this chapter, I'm going to share two unorthodox ways to convert Amazon shoppers into email subscribers:

1. Add an email signup offer to your book detail page

2. Create a "Bait Book" for readers to download on Amazon

Both of these techniques have been proven to help authors add more subscribers to their email list. I'll be candid by telling you not to expect gangbuster results. But, based on my own tests, I can attest to seeing a modest response. However, here's my perspective on trying any new method to grow your email list.

Most financial advisors will tell you that getting rich doesn't happen overnight. Instead, most people become wealthy be steadily adding a little money to their savings account every month and every year. Over time, those small deposits add up. The same principle applies to growing your email list. The techniques that I describe in this chapter may not produce huge results overnight. But, they are like adding small steady deposits that will accumulate to a much larger number over time. Best of all, these methods are free. So, there is nothing to lose by trying out these options.

Add an Email Sign-up Offer to Your Book Detail Page

This first chapter of this book talked about the importance of mastering your book detail page. No other place on Amazon's website gives you the direct ability to influence a reader's purchasing decision. Plus, your book detail page is the one place every reader must visit to buy your book.

Since everyone has to go to your book detail page, why not use that premium space to help build your email list?

Think about it. Where else do avid readers congregate in such huge numbers? No where else but Amazon. Therefore, when someone visits your book detail page, make them an enticing offer to join your email list. For example, at the top of your book description text, insert a short sentence with an offer for free e-books or an exclusive download if people go to your author website. For example, you could display:

Want a free e-book? Go to AuthorName.com/free-book
Want three free e-books? Check out AuthorName.com/free-books
Get a free video course at: AuthorName.com/video-course

Obviously, putting this offer at the top of your book detail page will get better results than burying the words at the bottom. The only place you know every shopper will see your offer is at the very top of the page.

If a reader likes the offer they see on your book detail page, they can copy the website address you display, paste it into their Internet browser, and go to that landing page on your website. At that landing page, people can join your email list and get the free books or videos that you're giving away. Plus, you can give that landing page a unique address in order to track how many people join your email list from Amazon.

Okay, I know what you're thinking, "Does Amazon allow authors to add promotions for their email list to a book detail page?"

Here's what I do know. Amazon frowns upon inserting active hyperlinks to other websites within your marketing text. But, notice how the examples above are not active hyperlinks. There is no "www" or "http://" displayed. Those words do not create a link that someone can click and leave Amazon's website. It's just a shortened name of your website that describes the landing page address to get a free offer.

In addition, I know authors who have been doing this technique for years without any complaints from Amazon. If it was against Amazon's policies, those authors would have been notified.

I would even suggest that this technique directly benefits Amazon. As authors add more readers to their email lists, they will send emails promoting new books to those readers in the future. When readers to receive those email announcements about new books, guess where they will go to purchase? Back to Amazon.

If you're an author who doesn't get much traffic to your website, then you must go to where the traffic already exists. What better place than Amazon?

I'm not suggesting this technique is right for every author. But, if you're looking for new ways to grow your email list for free, this option is worth considering.

In Chapter 4, I explained how to use your Author Central account to make improvements to your book detail page at any time. In this case, you can add new text that helps build your author email list.

Offer a "Bait Book" on Amazon

Another way to turn Amazon shoppers into email subscribers is using a tool that I call a "Bait Book." I know this term may sound strange. But, simply put, a Bait Book is:

A permanently free e-book placed on Amazon's website to attract readers in your genre and entice them to join your email list.

I use the term "Bait Book" in a light-hearted manner, because fly-fishing is one of my favorite hobbies. Using fishing as an analogy, your free e-book acts as "bait" that "hooks" readers into downloading content from you on Amazon. Once readers open your free e-book, they see a well-placed offer to get more free content from you if they go to your author website and join your email list.

Obviously, most readers must appreciate the content of your Bait Book to consider taking another step to join your email list. But, if they like your material, then you are adding highly-qualified readers to your list. That's because they jumped through two hoops to get on your email list:

1. The reader chose to download your free Bait Book on Amazon.

2. The reader chose to receive additional free content from you and join your email list.

You might argue that these steps only attract people who want everything for free. But, I would suggest that someone who willingly takes these two steps is sending a signal that they enjoy your material. Therefore, you are attracting readers to your email list who more likely to buy other books that you write.

Will everyone become an email subscriber and buy books? Of course not. But, at least you're attracting qualified leads to your email list, rather than cold traffic that is indifferent to your books. And, did I mention this approach is free plus it works for fiction and non-fiction?

Before I walk you through the steps of creating a Bait Book, let me demonstrate how the process works. Using the link below, take a look at my own Bait Book called, *Mastering Book Hooks for Authors.*

https://www.amazon.com/dp/B078L2FSFH

When you see *Mastering Book Hooks for Authors* on Amazon's website, notice that the price is set to free. Why am I giving away a free e-book? Am I crazy? No, giving away a free e-book presents a no-risk opportunity for people to try my material and get to know me better.

If someone has never heard of me or doesn't feel like risking money to buy my books, then my free e-book on Amazon encourages them to try my material. If I provide great content within the free e-book, which I do, then my free e-book converts a skeptical reader into a fan.

However, the critical component of a Bait Book goes beyond the free content you're giving away. The magic happens when readers see a compelling offer to get more free content if they join your author email list.

For example, when you click on the "Look Inside" feature of

Mastering Amazon for Authors, notice that a special offer is displayed at the beginning of the book right after the copyright page. The special offer says, "Free Gift for Authors." On this page, there is a picture and description of another free resource from me called "The Ultimate Book Marketing Plan Template for Authors." At the bottom of this page is a link to a landing page on my website to get this resource. View my landing page by using this link:

https://www.startawildfire.com/free-resources/book-marketing-plan-template

When readers go to my landing page, they see the same offer to get my "The Ultimate Book Marketing Plan Template for Authors." In addition, they see endorsements about me from bestselling authors and a box to enter their email address, join my mailing list, and access my free resource. Also, I clearly state that people will receive my weekly newsletter after entering their information. Once someone enters their email address and clicks on the button that says, "Get Your Free Copy," a thank-you page appears with a link to download my free "Ultimate Book Marketing Plan Template."

In case you're confused about everything that I just described, here's a quick recap:

1. I placed a free e-book on Amazon.
2. The free e-book encourages new readers to download and read my material.
3. Within the free e-book, readers see an offer to get more free content at my website.

4. To get the free content on my website, people must join my email list.
5. As people join my email list, I can market all of my books to them.
6. Once my Bait Book resides on Amazon, I can leave it alone and it works 24/7 going forward.

The obvious next question might be, "How many new subscribers does my Bait Book generate for my email list?" The results fluctuate. Sometimes, I only get a few per week. Other times, I get 1 – 2 new subscribers per day. Those numbers tend to be similar for my author clients who have implemented this same approach.

Creating a Bait Book is not a get-rich-quick-scheme where you can immediately retire to a private island and sip margaritas. Instead, the Bait Book technique is a strategic way to convert Amazon readers into email subscribers by giving them additional content for free. Plus, you can set up as many Bait Books on Amazon's website as you desire. You don't have to stop at one. You can create several Bait Books and increase your results at a faster pace.

If you have extra money to spend, you can also purchase Amazon ads to make sure more people see your Bait Book. Depending on your budget, buying ads to promote your Bait Book can be a wise investment.

Ultimately, here's why I'm a fan of Bait Books. Most authors, especially first-time authors, don't get many visitors to their author website. Even established authors can struggle to grow their website traffic. Thus, many authors wonder,

"How do I get more people to come to my website and join my email list?"

Here's the answer to that problem. Stop trying to get more traffic to your website. Go to where the traffic already exists. What is the largest source of online book reader traffic in the world? Amazon. With a Bait Book, you go to where the big traffic resides, rather than hoping and praying more traffic comes to your author website.

Even better, you can create a Bait Books for free using Amazon's Kindle Direct Publishing (KDP) platform. I'll walk you through the setup details in the next section.

Any author can utilize Bait Books to increase awareness of their published books and build their email list. It doesn't matter if you're a traditionally-published author or an indie author. It works great for fiction and non-fiction genres. Plus, it's effective for first-time authors and veteran *New York Times* bestsellers.

Frankly, the more successful you already are, the better results you can generate. A well-known author giving away a free e-book on Amazon will attract extra attention from readers. Ready to get started? The next section shows you how to do it.

How to Create a Bait Book on Amazon

I've broken down the Bait Book creation process into seven steps. When you want to give it go, follow these instructions:

Step 1 – Identify two separate pieces of free content to give away

Before you place a Bait Book on Amazon's website, you must plan ahead first. It takes two pieces of free content to ultimately get a reader to join your email list. The first piece of content is the Bait Book itself. The second piece of content is the free offer that you display inside the Bait Book. Do you see the difference? You need to two separate pieces of free content that work together in tandem.

Below is a list of ways to create attractive content that can work together. Your Bait Book can be a free e-book that includes an offer inside to get any of the following items at your author website:

1. A different complete e-book
2. Short story or novella
3. Access to a free video series
4. Action guide or bonus content
5. An "ultimate author sampler"

Notice how the two pieces of free content work together to get readers to join your email list. My Bait Book on Amazon, *Mastering Book Hooks for Authors*, works in tandem with a free offer inside for my "Ultimate Book Marketing Template for Authors," which is available at my author website.

Ideally, you want the two pieces of free content to relate to each other. Otherwise, readers might feel a disconnect between the free offer within your Bait Book and get confused. For example, it wouldn't make sense if my Bait

Book, *Mastering Book Hooks for Authors* promoted an offer to join my email list and get an e-book on how to fly-fish. Those topics aren't related to each other and that disparity would puzzle readers. To achieve success with the Bait Book technique, your two pieces of free content should relate to each other in some way. To make sure you follow what I mean, let me repeat some examples again:

- A fiction Bait Book could offer a free novella inside
- A nonfiction Bait Book could offer an action guide
- A nonfiction Bait Book could offer a free video series featuring similar content
- A fiction or nonfiction Bait Book could offer an "ultimate author sampler" inside

For established novelists who really want to "get jiggy with it," try these two options:

1. If you have a series of novels that contains 5 books or more, give away your first novel as the Bait Book. Then, inside the Bait Book, present an offer to get the second novel in your series for free if people join your email list. Then, you can focus on selling the remaining books in your series to highly qualified readers.

Successful indie authors, such as Adam Croft, use this approach effectively. Adam writes psychological thrillers under the Knight & Culverhouse series and has a large email list. He grows his list by offering a free Bait Book on Amazon entitled, *Too Close for Comfort*, which contains a link inside to get more free books at his author website if you join his VIP club.

2. If you don't have several novels in a series, join together with 3 – 4 other novelists in your genre and create a Bait Book that contain short stories from each author. At the end of each novella, you and the other authors can insert an offer to get another short story or free e-book at your author websites. By joining forces, you can work together to promote your Bait Book on Amazon and get more exposure.

Step 2 – Insert a free offer into your Bait Book manuscript

Let me be clear: Getting people to download your Bait Book by itself is not the goal. Otherwise, you're just giving away free content and getting little in return. Therefore, success with this technique hinges upon using the free offer within your Bait Book to attract email subscribers.

If you want to increase results, the cover art and marketing text for your free offer inside your Bait Book needs to look sharp. Use full-color images and present persuasive marketing text that entices readers to click on the link for your landing page.

Then, be sure to display the free offer for your second piece of content at the beginning and again at the end of your Bait Book. I recommend inserting the offer on the first page and again on the last page right after where it says, "The End." That way, you know readers will see it.

Showing your free offer in the front and back of your Bait Book maximizes the visibility with readers. If you only display your free offer once, or bury it at the back, many people may not see it. Therefore, all the work you did will be wasted.

Step 3 – Create a landing page for your free offer

Before you upload your Bait Book to Amazon, create a landing page on your author website for people to get your second piece of free content.

A "landing page" is a specific page on your website where people "land" and are persuaded to join your email list to get your free content magnet. This dedicated page is meant to minimize distractions and display only an image of your free offer from your Bait Book, compelling marketing text, influential testimonials, and a field for people to enter their email address. In other words, you get people's attention for your free offer in the Bait Book, but you send them to a landing page to close the deal and get their email address.

This should be a separate page from your Home page. On a landing page, display a picture of your Free Offer, such as the cover art for a free novella or e-book download. Include persuasive marketing text to close the deal. Then, display an email signup field where readers enter their email address.

Once your landing page is completed, insert the URL address as a link for it into your Bait Book manuscript. If you skip this step, then readers will see your free offer but have no way to access it. So, you need carefully follow my six steps in the right order to make this automated system work.

If you're unfamiliar with landing pages or need technical help, contact your webmaster or use a service dedicated to helping authors create landing pages, such as BookFunnel, Constant Contact, or Mailchimp.

From a legal standpoint, you must display clear language that tells visitors on your landing page that they are joining your author email list. New regulations in Europe, such as the General Data Protection Regulation (GDPR), were passed to prevent unlawful email spamming. Additional laws are being passed in the United States. These new regulations require authors to use language that tells people they are joining your email newsletter. If you don't display this language, you can face stiff fines.

For example, include language on your landing page that says, "Join my free newsletter to get e-books and updates from me." Make that text easy to see so that people won't be confused when they receive future emails from you.

Step 4 - Create a Thank You page to access your free offer

After someone enters their email address on your landing page, they're ready to receive your second piece of free content. Again, that may be a short story, a video series, or a downloadable e-book. Thus, the fourth step is to create a "thank you" page that appears after someone provides their email.

You can choose to give people your second piece of free content directly from the thank you page or send it to them via an automated email. The choice is yours to make. Either option has benefits.

If you provide a download link to access the free content on a thank you page, then your new subscribers can immediately enjoy their free gift. Most people would rather not wait to check their email inbox in order to receive the free content from you.

If you give away a free e-book to download, offer it in different file formats so that it can be viewed on more than one type of e-reader device. For example, a PDF file is a simple format that is most often preferred. However, some people would rather read your free e-book on their iPad, smartphone, or Amazon Kindle tablet. Those devices can only display e-books if they are in other file formats, such as an .epub or .mobi file. Providing these separate file formats is a nice touch for readers.

You can create PDF files for free using Microsoft Word. Or, you can convert Word files into .epub and .mobi files for free using an online service called Draft2Digital. Visit their website for details at: http://www.Draft2Digital.com

If you give away a free video course as your second offer, then you can put your videos on Vimeo or YouTube for free, list them as private, and embed them on your thank you page. Those steps help prevent people from sharing or pirating your videos without your permission.

If you'd like to pay for the convenience of letting someone else deliver your free e-book files to readers, check out a company called BookFunnel: http://www.BookFunnel.com

At the time of this writing, BookFunnel charges only $20 for a year to store 5 e-books on their servers with up to 500 downloads per month. If you need more downloads, you can get 5,000 downloads a month for $100 a year with unlimited books to give away. In my opinion, that's a great deal. Plus, BookFunnel manages all of the hassle to deliver your e-book to every type of e-reader device that exists. If your email subscribers have difficulty getting your e-book files onto their device, BookFunnel's customer service will talk with that person directly and handle the issue for you.

Step 5 – Place your Bait Book on Amazon

If you've followed along this far, you must be a book geek like me. So, you're ready for the fifth step, which is to add your Bait Book to Amazon's website. You complete this step by creating a free account with Amazon's Kindle Direct Publishing (KDP) service.

There isn't room in this book to explain all of the details to create an account and upload a Bait Book via KDP. But, I can assure you that Amazon's instructions are easy to follow and their customer service team is attentive. Use this link to create your free KDP account:

https://kdp.amazon.com/

Once your KDP account is active, you can upload the manuscript and cover art for your Bait Book to Amazon's website. KDP accepts common file formats for manuscripts, such as a Word document. Your book cover image should be uploaded as a JPEG or GIF files at a resolution of 300 pixels per inch or higher.

In addition, you will be able to add the marketing description for your Bait Book and set the appropriate categories, such as "mystery and thriller" or "writer's reference guides," based on your content.

After all of the information for your Bait Book is added to the KDP system, you can review how your Bait Book will appear using the Kindle Previewer feature before going live. Once your Bait Book looks good, Amazon asks you to set the price, such as $2.99, and then publish your book to Amazon's website. But, wait! Didn't I say that your Bait Book is supposed to be free on Amazon? Yes, go to the next step for the answer.

Step 6 – Ask Amazon to make your Bait Book free

If there's one tricky part to creating a Bait Book, it's the pricing issue. Technically, Amazon does not let authors sell permanently free e-books on their website. All e-books must have a price of $.99 or higher. However, there's a simple workaround to this problem. Amazon has a policy to always "price match" e-books sold by their competitors.

Therefore, you can force Amazon to make your Bait Book free by uploading the same e-book to Barnes & Noble or Apple iBooks and set your price to zero at those retailers. Now, some of you just thought, "Wait a second, this is getting complicated! How do I add my book to the other online retailers?" There is a simple solution to this problem.

Draft2Digital, the same company that lets you convert your Bait Book manuscript files for free, also lets you upload your Bait Book to other online retailers for free. Set up a free account with Draft2Digital. Then, upload your Bait Book manuscript to all of the other major online retailers and set the price to free, including Barnes & Noble, Kobo, iBooks, and WalMart.

Did you catch what I just said? Besides Amazon, Draft2Digital will enable your Bait Book to attract readers and email subscribers from several other online retailers! In other words, you can harvest new email subscribers from multiple sources. All because Draft2Digital does the extra work for you. Use this link to create an account:

http://www.Draft2Digital.com

Next, upload your Bait Book file to the Draft2Digital website, set the price to zero, and they will push it out to all of the non-Amazon retailers for you. Wait a day or two for your Bait Book to go live on Barnes & Noble's website as a free e-book. Then, go back to Amazon via your KDP account and take these steps:

1. Click the "Help" button at the top of the KDP dashboard.

2. On the "Help" page, scroll down and click the "Contact Us" button.

3. On the "Contact Us" page, you will see a menu that says, "How can we help?"

4. Click on the little button that says "Book Details."

5. On the drop-down menu, click the option that says "Pricing Your Book."

6. A new screen will appear that says "Ask your question here" with a field to type in your question for the KDP Customer Service team.

7. In the "Subject" field, enter "Request to price match my KDP e-book."

8. In the message window that appears next, enter a message that says,

"I'd like to request a price match for my KDP e-book, [Enter Your Title Here]. Here is the link to my e-book on Amazon.com: [Enter the direct link to your e-book on Amazon's website.]" Then say, "Here is a link to my e-book at Barnes & Noble:" [Insert the link where your Bait Book appears on the B&N website for free.]" Conclude your message by saying, "Thanks for price matching my e-book. I really appreciate it!"

9. Wait 48 hours and your Bait Book will appear as free on Amazon's website. The price will remain free on Amazon as long as it remains free on B&N or the other online retailers.

Be courteous with your communication to the Amazon KDP customer service team. They are doing you a huge favor by price matching your e-book and making the Bait Book strategy work on your behalf.

As a quick aside, do not be tempted to go around this step and set your Bait Book price to $.99 instead of $0.00. You might wonder, "Rob, why does that matter? If Amazon will let me sell books at $.99, why bother not make a little money on the side?" That approach is a mistake. If you set your price to $.99, then your Bait Book strategy will never reach its full potential. When your Bait Book is free, you will get more downloads, more exposure, and a better chance to drive more people to your email list.

Step 7 – Track your Bait Book results

The final step in the Bait Book process is to make sure you can track the results. You need to know how many new email subscribers join your list due to your Bait Book strategy. It would be a shame to do all of the steps I just described, drive Amazon readers to your author website, get them on your email list – but never know if the system is actually working. Don't trip at the finish line.

Here's the easiest way to know who joins your email list from your Bait Book. When you create the email signup form on your landing page, make sure that form is connected to a unique email list. For example, you can create a separate email list, such as "Bait Book Subscribers," with your email service provider. If you use MailChimp, Constant Contact, Convert Kit, or any other email service, you can create special lists to keep subscribers separate and track how they joined.

Another piece of helpful data is the reporting system from your Amazon KDP account. Within their system, you can track how many times your Bait Book is downloaded. If you get lots of downloads, such as hundreds or thousands per month, then you know your Bait Book is attractive to Amazon shoppers. If you only get a small amount of downloads, then your Bait Book may not be enticing. Pull it down and try a different type of Bait Book with more enticing content.

The numbers never lie. Your Bait Book will either drive consistent email signups or sit dormant on Amazon's website. If it sits dormant, kill it and start over with a stronger option. If it works well, consider buying Amazon ads to drive even more results.

When you combine data from Amazon's KDP platform along with your email service provider, you're able to see how many people download your Bait Book and how many actually join your email list.

The two techniques described in this chapter enable any author to lead Amazon readers into becoming email subscribers for free. Whether you write novels or nonfiction, these methods can work for you. Use the steps described in this chapter to create an automated system that generates these results:

1. Drive more reader traffic directly to your author website.

2. Add highly-qualified email subscribers to your list at no additional cost.

3. Enjoy a system that runs in the background 24/7 every day of the year.

4. Capture reader interest on Amazon and all other online retailers simultaneously.

Enjoy the excitement of fishing for new email subscribers on Amazon using your book detail page and an enticing Bait Book. Who knew book marketing could be so exciting?

CONCLUSION

Amazon's overwhelming dominance may present difficulties for publishers and competing retailers. But, their weight in the industry provides a unique benefit for authors. You can save a lot of time and money by focusing your marketing attention on the one retailer with the lion's share of book sales.

For instance, what if there were three other book retailers equal in strength to Amazon? That might be good for overall competition. But, you would have a lot more work on your hands as an author. After reading this book, imagine having to replicate the same strategies in several other places. Where would you find the time?

Amazon will eventually be usurped by another innovative company in the future. But, until that day comes, make sure you master the way your books appear where it matters most – on Amazon. As I mentioned at the beginning of this book:

Amazon sells more books than anyone else. If you want to sell more books, you must learn how to sell more books on Amazon.

I wrote *The Author's Guide to Marketing Books on Amazon* to help remove the guesswork and fear from promoting your books on their website. Now that we've reached the end, you know how to:

- Display language that turns shoppers into readers
- Attract more customer reviews for free
- Get your books noticed on Amazon's huge website
- Use Amazon ads to drive new readers to your books
- Build your author email list using Amazon's audience for free

Amazon's supremacy over the publishing industry may go unchecked for quite a while. Their power is something that you cannot control. But, you can control the way your books appear on Amazon and make sure more readers see that your books exist.

Use Amazon's advertising system to get your books noticed. Then, use the power of language to close the sale.

Thank you for purchasing this book to help guide your author journey. I wish all the best to you and your book sales!

Sincerely,

Rob Eagar

Wildfire Marketing

I trust that you found the instruction in this book helpful. If so, I'd be grateful if you took a few minutes to write a review on Amazon.

When you post a review, it makes a huge difference to help more readers find my books.

Your review would make my day!

Thank you,

Rob

MY FREE GIFT FOR YOU

Get 3 e-books to help jumpstart your book sales for FREE:

Find Readers and Sell Books on a Shoestring Budget

Mastering Book Hooks for Authors

The Ultimate Book Marketing Plan Template for Authors

Join my email newsletter and get these 3 e-books. Each resource can be downloaded as a file to your computer or added to any e-reader device. You will also receive my weekly e-newsletter packed with expert marketing advice for authors.

Download these 3 e-books for free today at:

https://www.startawildfire.com/free-ebooks-ag

ABOUT ROB EAGAR

Rob Eagar is one of the most accomplished book marketing experts in America. He has coached over 800 authors, advised top publishing houses, provided industry intelligence, and created numerous instructional resources for writers. His expertise has created these unique results for clients:

- Helped both fiction and nonfiction books hit the *New York Times* bestseller list
- Built and expanded email lists by over 25,000 subscribers in nine months
- Rebranded multiple authors who became *New York Times* bestsellers
- Developed bestselling book titles, marketing hooks, and book descriptions
- Revived a backlist book to hit the *New York Times* bestseller list after 23 years in print

Rob founded Wildfire Marketing, a consulting practice that has attracted numerous bestselling authors, including Dr. Gary Chapman, DeVon Franklin, Lysa TerKeurst, Wanda Brunstetter, Dr. Harville Hendrix, and Dr. John Townsend. In addition, he's consulted with imprints of the world's best-known publishers, such as HarperCollins (Thomas Nelson, Zondervan), Hachette (FaithWords), Simon & Schuster (Howard Books) and numerous small to mid-sized publishers.

Rob's expertise stems from starting out as a successful multi-published author. In 2002, he self-published his first book and generated a consistent six-figure income, long before the rise of social media and Amazon. His book was later purchased by a traditional publisher, sold over 50,000 copies, and remained on bookstore shelves for over 10 years.

His success attracted the attention of other authors who sought out Rob for marketing advice. This led him to found Wildfire Marketing in 2007 and provide marketing education to authors around the world. In addition, Rob partnered with Writer's Digest to publish the book, *Sell Your Book Like Wildfire,* and teach his online video course, *Mastering Amazon for Authors.*

Rob's industry-leading instruction can now be found in *The Author's Guide* series, a collection of books dedicated to teaching critical marketing topics, including:

The Author's Guide to Marketing Books on Amazon

The Author's Guide to Write Text That Sells Books

The Author's Guide to Email Marketing

Rob has served as a contributing writer and educator for Book Business Magazine, Digital Book World, Writer's Digest, and Reedsy. His national media appearances include interviews on the CBS Early Show, CNN Radio, and the *Los Angeles Times.* His background includes a marketing degree from Auburn University and 10 years of corporate sales experience before working full-time in publishing.

Rob is married to Ashley the Wonderful. When he isn't

consulting, you can find Rob fly-fishing for monster trout, breaking 40mph on his road bike, or loudly playing his drums. Ashley would prefer that he join her to quietly paint, work in their garden, or watch Jane Austen movies. They reside near Atlanta, Georgia.

For more details about Rob, his books, and his consulting services, visit his website at:

http://www.RobEagar.com

GET EXPERT HELP FOR YOUR BOOKS

Are you're tired of trying to figure out book marketing by yourself? What if an experienced coach guided you to the next level? Get personal help from one of the most accomplished experts in America.

Book Marketing Master Class

Become the hero of your own author story. The Book Marketing Master Class teaches how to master all key aspects of marketing a book. Whether you're a first-time author or a seasoned bestseller, Rob Eagar will show you how to:

- Attract more readers using the power of free content and email
- Create persuasive language, including hooks, titles, and back cover copy
- Construct a complete marketing plan to maximize the book launch sequence
- Turn your author website into a 24/7 sales machine
- Maximize advertising on Amazon and Facebook
- Connect with online influencers and turn media interviews into book sales
- Discover multiple ways to create new income from your book content

Rob's expertise applies to fiction and non-fiction, first-timer or bestseller, indie author or traditionally-published. He will personally teach you his proven marketing techniques and apply his instruction to your specific books, goals, and experience level. Work with Rob in person or receive instruction via live video sessions. Include your team and get everyone coached up at the same time. Receive follow-up access to ask Rob questions, hold you accountable, and request his review of your work. For details on the Book Marketing Master Class, visit:

https://www.startawildfire.com/consulting/book-marketing-master-class

Personal 90-Minute Author
Coaching Sessions

Are your book sales stagnant? Got a nagging question about book marketing or publishing? Ready to raise the bar on your author career? Reach your goals by talking directly with a world-class expert. Schedule a personal 90-minute author coaching session with Rob Eagar.

Individual coaching sessions include direct access to Rob to ask questions and learn how to improve your book marketing skills. Using live video screenshare technology, he will walk you step-by-step through everything you need to know. Get immediate answers to reach more readers, build a larger audience, sell more books, and increase your author revenue. For details about purchasing a 90-minute Author Coaching Session, visit:

https://www.startawildfire.com/consulting/author-consultation

OTHER BOOKS BY ROB EAGAR

The Author's Guide to Write Text That Sells Books

The Author's Guide to Email Marketing

For more information, visit:

http://www.RobEagar.com